LONG SHUI

LONG SHOT

The Triumphs and Struggles of an NBA Freedom Fighter

CRAIG HODGES

with Rory Fanning
Foreword by Dave Zirin

Haymarket Books
Chicago, Illinois

Published by
Haymarket Books
P.O. Box 180165
Chicago, IL 60618
773-583-7884
www.haymarketbooks.org
info@haymarketbooks.org

ISBN: 978-1-60846-607-8

Trade distribution:
In the US, Consortium Book Sales and Distribution, www.cbsd.com
In Canada, Publishers Group Canada, www.pgcbooks.ca
In the UK, Turnaround Publisher Services, www.turnaround-uk.com
All other countries, Publishers Group Worldwide, www.pgw.com

This book was published with the generous support of Lannan Foundation
and the Wallace Action Fund.

Cover design by Eric Ruder. Cover photo of Craig Hodges of the Chicago
Bulls during the 1991 NBA three-point competition at the Charlotte Coliseum in Charlotte, North Carolina. Copyright 1991 NBAE (Photo by An-
drew D. Bernstein/NBAE via Getty Images).

Printed in Canada by union labor.

Library of Congress Cataloging-in-Publication data is available.

10 9 8 7 6 5 4 3 2 1

CONTENTS

"YOU DON'T WANT TO BE LIKE CRAIG HODGES"

When I first started covering the NBA, back in 2003, I would ask players why more of them did not use their cultural capital to speak out on social causes. The answers varied, but I invariably heard, "You don't want to be like Craig Hodges." The answer was so puzzling. Many of these players were in elementary school when the long-distance marksman was draining three-pointers for the 1991 and 1992 champion Chicago Bulls. Yet his name lived on in the furtive whispers that agents and business managers would feed into their young clients' ears. "You don't want to be like Craig Hodges." I did not fully know what that even meant until I read this book—and learned from Mr. Hodges himself—what made his NBA legacy less about three-point championships or the Chicago Bulls' Michael Jordan dynasty than a cautionary tale of exile.

Long Shot exposes the fable of sports and politics history as a lie. There is a trafficked myth about the history of athletic activism, and it is one that serves only the kingpins of the sports-industrial complex. The myth goes something like this: the 1960s and 1970s saw a great deal of "athletic activism," as people like Muhammad

Ali, Billie Jean King, and Olympic protesters John Carlos and Tommie Smith raised awareness about injustices inside and outside the sports world. This brought about real change, and, coupled with profound rises in salaries, few athletes want to speak out today. They aren't rebels anymore. They're royalty.

There is certainly some truth to this history. The late 1960s and 1970s were absolutely a golden age for social justice–oriented jocks. And the explosion of salaries, which took place because of union battles for free agency, strikes, and the expansion of US sports through cable television as a global phenomenon, has of course been all too real. But what this history erases is that there have always been—even in the 1980s and 1990s—athletes who used their hyperexalted, brought-to-you-by-Nike platform to speak out about the world. In many respects, these athletes are the bravest of the brave because they chose to stand up in a period without mass movements in the streets and with a right-wing backlash against the movements of the 1960s permeating from DC. Because of that, these athletes paid the ultimate price for speaking out: banishment.

They were blackballed from the sports they served and were written out of the history books with a casual cruelty that would make Stalin envious. Yet their stories are vital not only because this is a resistance history worth celebrating. They also expose the true nature of the people whose hands are on the gears of the sports world. These plutocrats of play are a coterie of reactionaries who make billions off of the labor of the poor and the dreams of those in impoverished neighborhoods who may not even have PE at their schools—as city budgets go to building stadiums—let alone the rare athleticism and resources to make the pros.

Of all the exiled athletes, there is none more important in my mind than Craig Hodges. His story needs to be told and retold. Not only because it comprises a remarkable hidden history of what it was like to be a political athlete in an era when Nike had toppled Muhammad Ali as the new King of the World and undisputed champ. It matters because we now—finally—have a new generation of athletes trying to figure out how to leverage their star power to say something other than "Buy this flavored drink or swoosh-adorned crap." These changes are happening because of movements in the streets, but they have been ricocheting onto the field to dynamic effect. And this is especially the case in the NBA. Superstar players like LeBron James, Derrick Rose, and Dwyane Wade—among many others—have chosen to stand with the Black Lives Matter movement to say with bracing clarity that if they are worth cheering on the court, then their humanity and the humanity of their families need to be recognized off the court.

NBA players also had a critical role in finally toppling the openly racist "slumlord billionaire" owner of the Los Angeles Clippers, Donald Sterling (who, as a new owner, had a rookie on his San Diego Clippers team by the name of Craig Hodges). Superstars like Stephen Curry—who, as a young child, also makes an appearance in these pages—have stood with the victims of an anti-Islamic hate crime, and players have spoken out in support of LGBT rights so the world knows that the locker room is a safe space. It's been a head-spinning transformation for a league that for decades defined itself by its absence of politics, as every player wanted to be like the ultimate pitchman, who you'd better believe is in this book: Michael Jordan. But now those days are done. As Howard Bryant, columnist for ESPN and one of the most astute observers out there, said to me, "In the past, we would have been shocked if a player of LeBron's caliber had spoken out against police brutality. Now we become shocked when he doesn't."

As we go to press, the bar has been raised by San Francisco 49ers quarterback Colin Kaepernick's national anthem protest. He is standing up to police violence and racism, and for the very right of athletes to have a voice. Implicitly he stands in the tradition of Craig Hodges.

As players begin to find their voice, it is critical they realize that they are not "reinventing the wheel" and they do not have to go back fifty years to find athletes who felt the same passion for social justice that they shoulder. That is why the Craig Hodges story is so critical for every NBA player, every member of the media, and every NBA fan to read. It should also be read by anyone who has ever had to stand up in difficult circumstances and risk it all in order to be heard. It is time to remove Craig Hodges from exile status and place him where he has always belonged: on the short list of the activist athletes who stood tall, paid the price, and now live their lives perhaps scarred but without regrets. Read this book so a new generation of NBA players and fans will know his true story. Read this book so you can say not in a whisper but with crystal-clear confidence: "You *do* want to be like Craig Hodges."

Dave Zirin
Washington, DC, June 2016

PREFACE

I t was a humid morning in Chicago on Thursday, August 28, 2014. I had been working for Haymarket Books, a radical nonfiction book publisher in Chicago, for nearly four years by then. My book, *Worth Fighting For: An Army Ranger's Journey Out of the Military and Across America*, was on its way to the printer for a November release date. The book assesses my decision to leave the military after two tours to Afghanistan with the 2nd Army Ranger Battalion and then walk across the country for the Pat Tillman Foundation, in the hopes of recovering from my time in the military. I sat down at my desk, clicked on my computer, and looked for advance reviews. Nothing that day. I began scrolling through the forty or fifty emails that came through Haymarket's general information box. I clicked on an email with the subject line "My Book," a standard opener in a publishing house. "Peace. . . . My name is Craig Hodges," read the first line of the email. I did a double-take.

As a five-foot-two, barely one-hundred-pound fourteen-year-old, I could shoot three-pointers as well as any eighth grader in or around Chicago, or so I thought. Growing up in three different area suburbs, I followed every move the Bulls made during their six championship runs. Craig Hodges, more than Michael Jordan or Scottie Pippen, was my hero back then. I yelled, "Hodges for three!" every time Craig shot in a Bulls game, which I watched religiously. I'd yell the same words each time I shot in the playground. I wanted to be Craig Hodges.

I emailed Dave Zirin, the sports editor of the *Nation* and author of numerous books about sports and politics, after reading Craig's email.

Dave,

Craig Hodges, my childhood idol, is pitching Haymarket a book. Pretty damn cool. Do you know him? Thoughts on how we should proceed?

Thanks,
Rory

"Absolutely we should do it. Not even a question." Dave replied within minutes.

I emailed Craig and said Haymarket would be honored to see his book.

"I only have notes at this point and could probably use some help writing it. I noticed that Haymarket published *The John Carlos Story* by John Carlos and Dave Zirin, and I think I have a story similar to tell. Do you think Dave could help me tell my story, too?" Craig inquired.

I called Dave with the request.

"I am swamped with other work, as much as I'd like to there aren't enough hours in the day for me right now," Dave replied with regret.

"Do you think he'd let me write it with him?" I asked.

Dave had recently read and liked *Worth Fighting For.* "You should definitely ask him. . . . I wouldn't say that if I hadn't just read your book."

I called Craig and asked him if we could meet to discuss his story that Saturday.

"I'm making an appearance at a charity basketball game at St. Sabina's this weekend. If you are free we could talk about the book afterwards."

"Sounds great! See you there."

Craig and I met in the parking lot of a school on Chicago's South Side, where dozens of kids were shooting on outdoor hoops. Craig was immediately swarmed by the kids. He shot some baskets, took photos, and encouraged them to take their studies seriously. After shooting for a while, we walked into the school together and were greeted with a hug by Chicago civil rights icon Father Mike Pfleger.

"Craig! Great to see you! I have a bunch of things to do before the game. Would you mind sitting and waiting in the conference room by the gym? Other players should be here shortly."

Craig and I sat down and talked about his plans for the book. Ten minutes later, in walked Jabari Parker, the Chicago basketball phenom from Simeon High School and the Milwaukee Bucks' second pick in the first round of the 2014 draft. Following Parker was Joakim Noah, the Bulls' first-round draft pick in 2007 and two-time all-star. Next was arguably the greatest player Chicago has ever produced, Detroit Pistons Hall of Famer Isiah Thomas. Each of these players undoubtedly was used to being the center of attention, but expressions of reverence and respect transformed Parker, Noah, and Thomas as they noticed Craig.

"Mr. Hodges, it's an honor to see you again," said Joakim.

Isiah walked right up to Craig, looked him in the eyes for a long moment and gave him a bear hug. "Let's see where these guys are at," Isiah said to Craig almost immediately.

Craig and Isiah proceeded to ask Jabari and Joakim what both of them were doing to raise political awareness among other players in the NBA. "Don't let those big paychecks buy your silence," said Craig. "I understand it's easier said than done, but you two need to start talking amongst yourselves and the other players in the league. Time is running out for our communities. We are looking to you for your leadership right now." Isiah echoed the same points in his own style.

Jabari, who was only nineteen at the time, nodded his head and agreed, while acknowledging the pitfalls. "They try to keep us focused on the game, which makes conversations like that difficult," he said.

Joakim was more confident. He mentioned Noah's Arc Foundation, an arts- and sports-focused organization he'd founded to promote peace in violence- and poverty-stricken neighborhoods, an initiative he was clearly proud of. "As long as you are looking at the roots of poverty and racism and not just charity," said Craig. Joakim nodded.

Father Pfleger walked in and asked if the players would mind coming downstairs to talk to the media. Craig and I accompanied Jabari, Joakim, and Isiah to the press conference. The political charge, alive just moments before, seemed to die in front of the cameras as the players made careful comments about reducing gang violence through programs like Noah's Arc and Father Pfleger's charity basketball games. There was clearly a long way to go. Craig hadn't been expecting the press conference, and, citing another appointment, said that it was time we head out. I left St. Sabina's with a strong sense that Craig's story needed to be told.

In the months that followed Craig and I spent hours together going through every detail of his life. We realized that we'd lived parallel lives in some respects. He compared his decision to speak out in the pros to my decision to leave the Army Rangers as a war resister, and I understood where he was coming from. The book has been a natural fit from the beginning. I hope it inspires not just professional athletes to speak out against injustice in the world but anyone who is questioning whether or not to join the fight.

Rory Fanning
Chicago, May 2016

PROLOGUE

THE LETTER

The letter stared back at me in the days leading up to my visit to the White House. Resting open on my desk at home, it seemed to be saying, "Make sure you get this right because you'll only have one shot." The letter was eight double-spaced pages. It had endured dozens of rewrites in my attempts to express the lessons taught to me by my family, teachers, and community. Its first line read:

> The purpose of this note is to speak on behalf of the poor people, Native Americans, homeless, and most specially the African Americans who are not able to come to this great edifice and meet the leader of the nation in which they live.

On October 1, 1991, four months after my basketball team, the Chicago Bulls, won its first NBA championship, we visited 1600 Pennsylvania Avenue to receive the official thumbs-up from President George H. W. Bush. The Bulls would be the first NBA squad to shoot hoops on an outdoor basketball court on the White House grounds.

Determined to make the most of this chance to speak truth to power, I aimed to inform the president of the United States that

I was not only an athlete but a descendant of slaves, a child of the Black liberation movement, and a man willing to fight to make the world a better place for the African American population. I would use this visit to help escalate discussions of rising incarceration, reparations for slavery, the causes of street violence, and the plight of Black people in the United States to the highest office in the land, on behalf of the community that raised me.

Nineteen ninety-one had been one hell of a year: no more Soviet Union; the first US war in Iraq; and, as of March, the tape of Rodney King's beating by four Los Angeles police officers filling television screens across the country. And, for me, in my hometown of Chicago, the place that raised me and the place where I played ball, 922 people were murdered in 1991 alone.[1] Thirty-two percent of African Americans in Illinois lived below the poverty line, and America housed more Black prisoners than South Africa did under apartheid.[2] The conditions of my people were deteriorating rapidly. I knew that I would hardly have the chance to debate President Bush in the Rose Garden—and even if I did, I wouldn't be able to say everything I wanted to.

But I did have my letter. On the bus, on the way to the White House, I told Tim Hallam, the public relations director for the Bulls, that I'd written something to give to the president. He looked at me like I was out of my damn mind. Then he said it would be best if he handed the letter to Bush's press secretary. I had planned to give the president the letter myself, but I wanted to ensure it was read, so I followed protocol and gave my letter to Tim.

I also told some of my Bulls teammates on the bus. By this point they were used to my political outspokenness, and, as usual, the response was something like, "Man, you're crazy, Hodge." In the NBA—even though 75 percent of the players were Black—you still couldn't be upfront that helping Black people was part of your personal mission. Race-based charity or political action had to happen in secret. Subtle and not-so-subtle pressures from management and media prevented many of us from upsetting the corporate order of the league. A whole lot of players knew more should be done for the communities most of us came from, yet the fear of losing our spot always knocked out the urgent need to fight racism and structural poverty. But not for me.

And that's why, as we got to the White House, all my teammates, out of respect, wore wearing suits. I also wore an outfit out of respect. I was wearing my precious dashiki.

My teammates were well-acquainted with this dashiki, a special white and flowing African ancestral garment. I wore it to games before getting into uniform, and I was a bug in the ear of the Bulls' young stars Horace Grant and Scottie Pippen to wear one also. They'd laugh—not unkindly—and say, "That's your thing, man." But as long as I was in the NBA, I was set on representing my African heritage. I was raised to know that my history was unwritten, so if the books weren't going to represent it, I would. I felt that if I was going to be in the White House, I had to communicate my Black history even without speaking. There was no question I would be showing up to 1600 Pennsylvania Avenue in a dashiki.

When we got to the White House, one of the first people to greet us was a hyper, overcaffeinated sports fan, who we quickly learned was the president's son, George W. Bush. He was bouncing around like a kid, but when he saw me in my dashiki he froze and did a double-take. (This was a look I would recognize years later, when, as president, he dodged a shoe thrown at him by an Iraqi journalist.)

"Where are you from?" George W. asked me, slowly and loudly, as if I might not speak his language.

"Chicago Heights, Illinois," I answered.

He looked amazed. "Well, that's an awesome garment!" Bush Jr. replied. I smiled, thanked him in English, and walked with the rest

of the team to the South Lawn of the White House, where Bush Sr.
and his wife, Barbara, waited for us.

There was one notable absence from the team on the visit that
day. During the finals against the Lakers, when it was all but assured
that we had the championship sewn up, Michael Jordan—who everyone thought did not have a political bone in his body—said, in
the locker room, "I'm not going to the White House. Fuck Bush. I
didn't vote for him." True to his word, Jordan didn't join us that day.
The *Chicago Tribune* and the *New York Times* wrote mildly critical
articles about Jordan's decision to snub the president, but most of
the media ignored the move.

Why? Jordan raked in $15 million a year in endorsements,
was a popular guest on *Saturday Night Live*, and had highways in
North Carolina named in his honor. Jordan had transformed the
game of basketball to the point that people would pay thousands
of dollars a ticket to sit courtside and watch a bunch of brothers
run up and down a painted court and put a ball through a hoop.
It was best not to draw too much attention to such things as having the league's cash cow boycott a visit to the White House. The
"Jordan Rules" weren't just the Detroit Pistons' secret formula for
stopping MJ. They were also the rules of the *game* that didn't apply
to Jordan.

The team set up on the green half court on the southwestern
corner of the South Lawn. President Bush had dedicated the half
court the previous April, after attending a midnight basketball
league game in Maryland. He was so impressed that he designated
the midnight basketball league, with its aim of drawing young Black
kids off the streets during peak crime hours of 10 p.m. to 2 a.m., as
one of his national "thousand points of light." (Midnight basketball
leagues are great, but believe me, they don't represent a serious approach to curbing gang violence.)

B. J. Armstrong was the first to pick up a basketball. He made twelve straight bank shots from about ten feet, set on breaking Grant Hill's record of ten straight bank shots when he'd helped inaugurate Duke University's court a few months earlier. (You can't have a Dukie with the record. That's just the truth.)

"He can really shoot," said Bush Sr. to our coach, "The Zen Master," Phil Jackson.

"Yes, he can, but he isn't our best shooter," Phil said, as he pointed to me.

"I'm too clean, Coach," I said with a smile, nodding to my white dashiki. B. J. tossed me the ball anyway. I began draining shots from about twenty-four feet; I think I hit nine in a row.

The president was impressed. "Bar, did you see these guys?" Bush Sr. said to the First Lady. I had never felt more joy shooting a jump shot than I did on that White House court. Having delivered a letter to the US president on behalf of my people, after winning the first NBA championship for my hometown, I felt I was repping all that I held sacred and dear—in that moment I was the fullest, realest expression of Craig Hodges.

As we left the court, I noticed the ball sitting alone. I picked it up and asked, "Mr. President, would you sign this?"

"Of course," he said.

I decided to seize the moment. "I wrote a letter for you. Your press secretary has it. I hope you have a chance to look at it."

"Thank you. I look forward to reading it, Craig," said the president, in his New England–Texas hybrid accent, as we walked off the court together.

Getting the message to him mattered to me. I wanted to put the president on notice and show him how desperate things were getting in the poorest, Blackest neighborhoods in America. These issues wouldn't be ignored by me while I stood on the grounds of one of the most powerful buildings in the world.

Here's an excerpt of what I wrote, as an opener:

Dear Mr. President:

> ....This letter is not begging the government for anything.... but
> 300 years of free slave labor has left the African American com-
> munity destroyed. It is time for a comprehensive plan for change.
> Hopefully this letter will help become a boost in the unification
> of inner-city youth and these issues will be brought to the fore-
> front of the domestic agenda.

Tim Hallam, the Bulls' PR director, for reasons that I still don't understand, shared my letter with the press. He certainly didn't have to do that, but I was glad he did. Why not? If I'm going to do it, let the world know! The *Chicago Tribune,* the *Sun-Times,* and other outlets reported on what I'd written.

As I was raised to believe that writing political representatives was a normal and healthy part of living in a democracy, I left the White House feeling like I'd just aced Civics 101. I was more than just an athlete. I was a young man eager to continue to use the platform I'd earned as a professional athlete to draw attention to those who couldn't play in the NBA. I'd soon learn, however, that the overlords of the league had other plans for me and that my freedom of expression had serious limits—limits that would cost me my livelihood.

This is my story.

CHAPTER 1

CHICAGO HEIGHTS

I was born June 27, 1960, in Chicago Heights, Illinois. Just a few months earlier, students had started sit-ins at the segregated lunch counters in Greensboro, North Carolina. It was like I couldn't wait to pop out and get with them. Chicago Heights is thirty miles from the downtown Chicago Loop and twenty-two miles from Gary, Indiana. So in the span of just fifty-two miles, you can see the transition between two different worlds—and there we were, caught in the middle. Chicago Heights was a stop on the Underground Railroad, and two houses right near my own home were part of this abolitionist network. History was all around me. As a kid I liked to say, "Chicago may be a railroad town, but Chicago Heights is an Underground Railroad town."

When I was growing up, my reality was defined by segregation. Black folks lived on the east side of the tracks, in older, worn-down townhomes, while the white folks lived in two-story Georgian and Victorian style homes on the west side. We were literally on "the wrong side of the tracks." There were no official Jim Crow segregation laws on the books, but there was rampant redlining—the practice of refusing loans or services to people who lived in areas considered a "poor financial risk," usually African American neighborhoods. This was economic planning aimed at keeping segregation hidden in plain sight.

I attended Dr. Charles Gavin Elementary School. And I'm so proud of that fact. The light bulbs flickered, the floors were dirty, the schoolbooks were usually shared, and the classrooms always felt crowded, so it's not the conditions of the school that make me proud. It's the name.

My school wasn't called Gavin when I started. Its name back then was Benjamin Franklin Elementary School, but Ben Franklin didn't mean much to us kids. Not as much as Dr. Charles "Buddy" Gavin.

Dr. Gavin was one of the first African American orthopedic surgeons in the United States. He attended the University of Illinois in the 1950s, and, after earning his medical degree, he returned to the Heights to begin his general practice. He made door-to-door house calls, just like in the movies. He understood that Black folks worked when they could find work, and tended to be home at odd hours. Always on the move, Dr. Gavin could often be seen walking down the street with his doctor's bag, waving, like a Norman Rockwell painting. Everyone on the east side of our town loved him. He looked you in the eye when he spoke, his voice was calm and reassuring, and you relaxed in his presence. Even at a young age I knew how hard Dr. Gavin worked, but his stress never showed. He would pick up his stethoscope or otoscope deliberately, never as if he needed to finish in order to go somewhere else. Dr. Gavin also provided his services for free when folks couldn't afford to pay him. There were no insurance checks with him.

What made the doctor so special in my mind, though, was not just his kindness, generosity, intelligence, and his patience, but rather his decision to live and practice medicine in Chicago Heights. He could have gone anywhere and found a regular stream of patients that would pay for every visit, but instead he chose to return home to help those who needed him most. He didn't abandon his roots when he had the chance.

Those living on the west side of town—the "right" side of the tracks, the side of town with trimmed lawns and tight haircuts—had a different view of Dr. Gavin. He had purchased a fixer-upper on the west side with money he had scraped together through his medical practice. When Dr. Gavin wasn't seeing patients, he was hammering away at wooden boards, intent on building a beautiful home for his family. He insisted on repairing the house—which seemed to need a lot of work—himself, so it took a while, long enough for everyone on the east side to know at any given time what stage of the process he was in. He enjoyed discussing the details of the plumbing, the roofing, the wiring, all of it.

One day, as Dr. Gavin's house was nearing completion, it caught fire. My mom and aunts raised the subject of the fire on a few occasions, always with furrowed eyebrows. They believed it was arson. I didn't know what "arson" meant at that age, only that it sounded cruel. The circumstances of the fire were suspicious, but no one was ever fingered for the crime. The house was saved, and Dr. Gavin kept building. He eventually finished and the Gavin family settled in. The sense of accomplishment Dr. Gavin felt after the house was complete could be seen a mile away. It was not only the house that brought him joy but also the belief that Chicago Heights could be integrated, the trust that humans could live together as equals. Less than a year after his family moved in, the house went up in flames again. This time it couldn't be saved, and the beautiful home that a beautiful man restored by hand burned clear to the ground. Even my Grandma Dorothy, who was quiet as a church mouse when it came to these types of matters, pounded the table in disgust upon hearing the news. The police said arson was difficult to prove, and no one was prosecuted. Maybe it was an accident. I don't think it was.

Dr. Gavin died at the young age of forty-four in 1971, about two years after his house went down in flames. He seemed like such an elder to me at the time, but that's all he was. Forty-four. I was eleven at the time. The entire community mourned the loss. Dr. Gavin was a survivor, a fighter, someone who we thought would live forever. They said it was his heart, but everyone knew it was the stress of all that work helping others, and the burning of his house, that had brought him down.

After Dr. Gavin died, the kids at school and I decided we wanted to change the name of our school to Dr. Charles Gavin Elementary. When I look back, we were motivated by a deep sense of loss, but on another level it was about justice. I think some of us who campaigned to have the school name changed knew it would bother those who may have been responsible for Dr. Gavin's house burning down. Benjamin Franklin was their hero. Dr. Gavin was our hero.

We gathered signatures on a petition, walking door to door along the tree-lined streets and cracking sidewalks of Chicago Heights, and made announcements in each classroom of the school. We did this on our own, but our families supported us. In hindsight, it's clear that they planted the seeds and encouraged us. "How did your petition drive go today?" my mom would ask after school, clearly interested. I liked telling her how many signatures we collected. Still, it was a kid-led movement and I was proud to help lead it. It gave me a buzz to rally others behind a cause, and it seemed to come naturally.

Changing the school name was surprisingly easy because most of the kids supported it. The administrators of the school—who were all white—may have had their reservations, but it was hard to argue against such an overwhelming show of unity on the part of the student body. Maybe they knew something we couldn't prove. Either way, I learned early that change was something that happened only if we made it happen.

* * *

A village raised me—a loud, busy, packed village. The whole world seemed to live in my Grandma Dorothy and Grandpa Bruce's house: my grandparents, my mom, her eight brothers and sisters, and my older sister, Lori. Including me, that was thirteen of us, and that's just the folks who slept under that roof. We had a regular stream of neighbors stopping by Grandma Dorothy's yellow kitchen, ornamented with her treasured bell collection. They came by to talk, to ask for help paying bills, or to be fed. Grandma Dorothy was famous for her smothered steak, mashed potatoes, green beans, and cornbread. She made it a rule never to turn anyone away, at least not without a thorough discussion of the matter, which was usually about why someone needed to stop drinking so damn much. More often than not the cast of characters who stopped by Grandma Dorothy's for food left with more than they'd asked for.

When we weren't eating in the kitchen, my uncles, my friends, and I played basketball in it. Two parallel pipes ran just below the ceiling, and we'd squeeze a cardboard box between them, with top and bottom removed—our basket. We'd shoot with balled-up socks, crumpled-up newspapers. We managed to fit six or seven players in the kitchen for marathon games of three on three. My grandma never seemed to mind the wild games. She even cheered us on.

Even with the regular flow of people into our smallish three-bedroom project townhome, I never considered my house cramped. My mom, aunts, uncles, and grandparents gave me the most important space of all: those six inches between my ears. I was free to think my own thoughts and say what was on my mind. My family always encouraged debate and discussion. They never forced me to subscribe to a particular religion. "Figure out where and why the Black folks are congregating," my mom would say. "You have to know what your people are up to." She believed in God but mostly believed in the heart of her people. Our home's open-minded atmosphere made me feel like I didn't have to hide. I could be me.

In our house, our sports heroes were also what were called "race men": people who stood their ground on issues like racism and injustice in America. On TV and in the papers, Muhammad Ali, Curt Flood, Jim Brown, Tommie Smith, and John Carlos were forcing Main Street, USA, to listen. The lesson was clear: athletic skills were one thing, but speaking tough truths is what made you a hero. Without that, you were incomplete. Sports had made a crack in the wall for Blacks, but we admired those who tried to break the walls down. I don't remember a thing about who won what at the '68 Olympics in Mexico. I do remember being eight years old and seeing that image of Tommie Smith and John Carlos raising their fists in a Black Power salute, with their black gloves, open jackets, and beads. They had no fear. And, more important, my uncles looked up to them—and you'd better believe I looked up to my uncles.

I was going to be one of those political athletes. But I needed smarts—not just sports—to do it right. My Aunt Diane and my mom were serious students. Aunt Diane's books—biology, geometry, and history, and the novels she read just for fun—were stacked high on the living room coffee table most nights. A bolt of lightning could crack through the ceiling and she would keep reading. People could be debating something right behind her and she wouldn't look up. After finishing with her assignments, she would interject her thoughts on the question of the evening, making it clear to all she had followed everything that had been discussed.

My mom, Ada, was the same but more stubborn. Her high school tried to force home economics classes on her. She wasn't having it and insisted on taking business classes; for a Black woman, that was unheard of at her school. Taking business meant learning shorthand. My mom said, "They just assumed I couldn't do it.

But that only made me work harder." She was the only African American in her class to graduate with shorthand skills, and she maintained a lot of pride in that. After graduation she accepted a job in an office in the Chicago Loop and held that same job for thirty-five years.

My mom took me to my first protest. It was August 1965, and Martin Luther King Jr. was in town helping organize the Chicago Freedom Movement to challenge unfair housing and job practices, as well as unequal education for Blacks. My mom insisted I march alongside the protestors. It was important to her that I connect with the struggle at an early age. I was only five years old. I don't remember much from that day, other than sore feet by the end of it. But she tells me I didn't complain about the long march one bit.

Then there was my Aunt Edna. She was the first person in our family to attend college. After graduation she taught first through seventh grades—all of them. You have to have a Swiss Army knife of teaching skills to be able to pull that off. She was my teacher in a few grades and was always on me about the books. She seemed to be clairvoyant when it came to my activities outside the house, too. One evening when I was in fifth grade, friends and I were throwing rocks at the neighbors' window. The streetlights were nearly ready to flicker on, and my friends Chris Alexander, Barry Lee, and I decided we were going to try to break something, anything, before we went home. I suggested the neighbors' window because I was sure they were away. I ran up and threw a rock, and it bounced back—*boom*! It shot right back at me. Undeterred, I picked up another rock, ran up, and threw it—*crash*! I fled.

Winded, I sat with my friends on Chris's front steps. Chris told me he'd seen a shard of glass hit a little kid in the neck after the window broke. I believed him. Later, as I lay in bed, I shook with fear the rest of the night. Had I killed someone? I must have said the Lord's Prayer a thousand times that night and promised God I would never throw rocks again if that little boy was OK.

Somehow my Aunt Edna found out about it the next morning at school. On my lunch break she came up to me and said, "Now, what were you up to last night, Craig?" She seemed calm considering I thought I killed a boy. I told her and started crying. "I know that isn't you, Craig. Promise me you won't do it again," she said, sternly and coolly.

"I promise," I said, sniffling and wiping away the tears.

We restored that window and I did extra chores around the house to pay my mom for the costs. It was dumb, but I can't help but think if a young Black kid did the same thing today, they couldn't get away with an apology and paying it back. They'd probably get a criminal record. I swear it feels like this country eats its own children.

While working and raising us, Aunt Edna and Mom also made time to found a civil rights group. It was called the Steering Organization Coordinating Community Action (SOCCA). They both had good jobs, but they also acknowledged that they were the exception in our community. In my elementary school, where Aunt Edna taught, they paid white women twice as much as Black women. And the white women, in turn, were paid a much smaller percentage of what white men made for the same work.

My aunt used to say, "They act like white teachers deserve combat pay for teaching Black kids." The mass flunkings incensed her, too. "They held nearly my entire class back this year. Now, I know they weren't all slow," I remember her saying. Fighting for equal education and fair pay for teachers motivated them to organize SOCCA, and they spent two or three nights a week trying to grow the organization.

Their group prioritized knocking on doors in the hopes of gathering enough signatures to stop the federal practice of redlining. They knew ending these discriminatory policies would require more than signatures, so they coordinated marches and sit-ins as well. As part of this push against redlining, they wanted to "ban the box." Until 1970, appraisals for homes had a little box that had to be checked if Blacks, Jews, or other minorities lived in a given neighborhood. This informed the banks and the federal government what races lived in a given community. There were varying degrees of economic penalties on the value of a house, depending on the racial makeup of the neighborhood. If the "Negro" box was checked, the neighborhood was expected to see the greatest decline in property value. Banks wouldn't lend, and Federal Housing Authority (FHA) loans wouldn't be approved in these neighborhoods. This is how the United States maintained legal segregation without official Jim Crow laws in the North, and one of the reasons Malcolm X used to say, "As long as you are south of the Canadian border, you are in the South."

My mom and aunt also blamed redlining and segregation for what happened to Dr. Gavin. Despite being a respected doctor, Dr. Gavin's skin color alone would drive property values down. He got around redlining because he didn't need a loan to buy his home, but it wasn't like that for most African Americans. Blacks had to live somewhere; we needed loans but couldn't get them, so we ended up buying homes at inflated prices in the same concentrated neighborhoods under "contract," or a private loan with almost no legal oversight and exorbitant interest rates. These homes purchased on contract required big down payments. If one payment was missed—this usually happened because a repair was needed—the family, or I should say *families*, would be kicked out of the house. Ultimately, what would happen was a whole bunch of people would have to move into a house just to pay the mortgage. Of course, at the inflated interest rates, paying for upkeep was almost impossible, so the houses usually fell apart. White people would drive by these places and view them from the curb and say, "Look what happens when Blacks move into a neighborhood."

White people didn't want their property values to go down, so they fought to keep Black people out, in some cases even—as I believe happened to Dr. Gavin—resorting to arson.

Even today, Chicago and certain suburbs like Chicago Heights are still extremely segregated and run-down in largely African American areas. You can't understand why these cities and towns look the way they do without knowing the history of redlining. This is why my mom and aunt fought.

I remember the fire in their belly when they came home after attending meetings with Dr. Martin Luther King Jr., after he'd visited Chicago. King, of course, was struck down in 1968, but by 1970, redlining had been made illegal. I know my mom and my aunt take great pride in their petition drives and marches that helped end it. Just as I'm proud to say I helped rename my elementary school Dr. Charles Gavin Elementary.

CHAPTER 2

SHOWING UP

I was skinny and bony as a kid, yet somehow I ended up playing catcher on all my little league teams. Usually the catcher is the big, squat kid. I may not have been big, but I could catch the ball as well as anyone. I also hit from both sides of the plate. I played baseball because it was the sport that everyone in the neighborhood was into at the time. We had nine gloves that we shared. If we didn't have a baseball we used a tennis ball, or we'd run down to the corner store and buy a rubber ball. In the eight years I spent playing baseball, there is one game I will never forget. That's because it was the game I didn't play.

It was the summer between fifth and sixth grade, and we were in the league championship. Raymond McCoy was pitching for the opposing team. Raymond had a strong arm and was considered the best athlete in Chicago Heights. (Texas A&M began recruiting him to play basketball while he was in eighth grade.) I knew I would struggle to hit the ball. I was also a little scared that one of Raymond's fastballs would hit me in the face. Butterflies were fluttering in my stomach for days in the lead-up to the championship.

The morning of the game I told my mom I was sick and hid in my bedroom. The team would figure a way to win without me, I thought. The clock ticked by on the desk next to my bed. The game was on a few blocks away. Warm summer air and a sense of relief blew through my room. Whatever happened in that game, I wouldn't be responsible.

A few hours later I heard someone sprinting up the stairs, then a knock on my bedroom door. It was Ernie Harper, the team captain. We called him "Banks," after our favorite Cubs player, Ernie Banks. He started talking to me through the closed door in his unnaturally deep voice. "Hodge. You ain't sick. Let me in."

"I'm sick. I'll catch up with you tomorrow, Banks."

He walked in anyway. "Hey, man, all you had to do was suit up and sit behind that plate. We coulda won. If you showed up and we lost at least we would have known what we could've done. But we'll never know now because you weren't there."

I started to feel guilty but stayed mute, staring at my baseball trophies from the previous year. He got up to leave, and I said, "Check you later."

"Yeah, man," Ernie replied, with resignation in his voice. "Never be afraid to compete, Hodge."

That was the first time I can remember feeling like I let my friends down. What was the point of being part of a team if I was going to be a no-show when my friends needed me most—better to stay in your room all the time. Ernie's advice haunted me. Since then I've always shown up, no matter what. I began arriving at games and practices early. I never wanted someone to say what Banks said to me again.

* * *

When I wasn't playing baseball you might assume I was playing hoops. But I was on the tennis courts with my aunts in the park. They were off-the-chain good: like Althea Gibson in the flesh. (Similar to the "race men," Althea Gibson, the first Black Grand Slam champion, was a goddess in our household.) My Aunt Pat taught me how to hit through the ball and control where it landed on the other side of the net without slowing down my swing. I could have played tennis in high school but it never felt like it was an option. Other than my aunts, no one I knew played the sport. My aunts were good enough to have played in college, but Title IX wasn't passed until 1972, after they'd all graduated. They didn't have the chance.

Aunt Pat, who never missed a major tennis match on TV, called me downstairs one afternoon when I was about eleven or twelve years old. "Craig, you gotta see this guy," she yelled from the couch. "He is so good. And look at that afro!" She was watching Arthur Ashe, the first and only Black man to win the US Open, in 1968, and the singles title at Wimbledon, in 1975. What struck me most about Ashe, even at my young age, was how he embraced his Blackness. There was a power and a grace not only in his swing but also in his appearance. I hadn't been one to watch tennis on TV, but after that day, sitting with Aunt Pat, it became our thing to make sure we always watched Ashe.

I was mesmerized by the man. He stayed composed in tense matches, to my eternal amazement. Never appearing rattled, he meditated right there on the court, in front of the world. He showed me that staying calm in nerve-wracking situations was an art and a spiritual pursuit. Ashe always maintained a connection to his inner peace, which inspired me to take meditation and prayer seriously. In addition to the afro, Ashe wore large, spellbinding African beads around his neck. The beads were more than just fashion—they were history, a symbol representing something I didn't quite understand at the time. Still, I wanted my own set.

Ashe was more than just his appearance and athletic success. Racism directly affected Ashe's career. He wasn't allowed to play in the 1969 South African Open because he was Black. He used his public visibility to change the world by empowering Blacks internationally, acting not simply through charity but through political action. When he joined the boycott of South Africa in 1977 he helped shape the broader anti-apartheid and boycott movement in sports. Some say he wasn't radical enough. The man was arrested for protesting the US treatment of refugees from Haiti, and for protesting the apartheid regime in South Africa. Arthur Ashe did more than talk; he led.

My Grandpa Bruce coached baseball, football, and track on the east side of Chicago Heights. He was the first Black track captain at Bloom High School, in 1928. Originally from Lincoln, Nebraska, Grandpa Bruce focused on track because he wasn't allowed to play contact sports in Lincoln. He explained that, at that time, Blacks weren't allowed to touch white folks. He never talked much about his early childhood, before the family moved to Chicago Heights in the late 1920s. Granddad was an excellent athlete, and he could play any sport. I knew he wondered what things would have been like if he'd been able to play interracial sports, but he didn't like to look back if he could help it.

Granddad named his eldest son Larry, after #14, Larry Doby, the second African American to play major league baseball and first in the American League, playing for the Chicago White Sox. Fourteen would be my number, too, in the NBA. Baseball was my granddad's first love. It was from my granddad that I learned that guys like Jackie Robinson hadn't necessarily been the best Black baseball players at the time. They were the ones who had enough talent to play in the majors but, equally important, had the strength to let hate roll off their backs, at least publicly. This is not an easy combination to come by. I used to think about all the talent who never made it to the white major leagues. It seemed like such a damn waste.

My Uncle Larry was scouted by many of the major league baseball teams all through high school. He was on his way to the pros until he broke his arm senior year. I watched his dreams shatter with that arm. My granddad wouldn't let Larry feel sorry for himself, though. He and Grandma always stressed academics and a hopeful mind-set. Even though they both loved sports, they knew there was more to life. Uncle Larry picked himself up and held down a well-paying government job for thirty years before he retired. Usually we only hear the stories of failed athletes that end in tragedy. They don't have to.

It was my Uncle Bruce who taught me to shoot hoops. He'd take me to the courts at Franklin Elementary School—this was before we changed the name to Gavin—and he'd stand there and throw elbow after elbow, and slap my hand as I tried to get the ball off. Initially it hurt, and I'd be distracted by the pain and miss. Uncle Bruce kept at it. I grew determined to show him that I had the mental toughness to fight through the pain. Shooting while being fouled became second nature. This would prove to be an invaluable lesson for the pros. He was teaching me how to create separation to get off my shot, how to work in a crowd. I had a naturally quick release but the space I learned to make for myself was what let me see the basket most clearly.

All the practice in creating space paid off. I started in the backcourt on the sixth-grade team when I was just in fifth grade. When I was trying out, Uncle Bruce told me, "You can never get cut." His words were gold to me. There was no other way if my Uncle Bruce said it was so. It wasn't pressure: it was confidence. Raymond McCoy, the best athlete in Chicago Heights—the pitcher I was so scared to face that I stayed home—started in the backcourt with me. Raymond played point guard, and together we were unstoppable. A basketball prodigy, Raymond had a sixth sense about where the open man was. He would drive and kick it out to me and I'd shoot the ball from the corner. When I was in the pros I'd often remember doing a move for the first time—faking someone out on the baseline or something like that. I'd look back and think, wow, Raymond was showing me that move in sixth grade, and it stuck in my head somehow. We played together and against each other in many games through high school.

There was a hierarchy of courts in my neighborhood. Franklin/Gavin was for the younger kids. There was Lincoln for the older kids. The top of the heap were the courts on Martin Luther King Jr. Street. There were two courts on King, and you had to be serious if you wanted to play on the big court. There was no room for goofing off. These games were intense. I was running on the top court at King by my sophomore year.

One day at King, that intensity spilled over into real danger. I was fourteen, cleaning up the court as my summer job with the park district, when I saw a guy take a hard foul. He got up and started beating the guy who gave him the foul. He really pounded him. The fouler got up, all bloody, and ran off the court. About an hour later he came back with a gun, shooting. He emptied an entire clip, firing at anything and anyone. Like a bag full of dropped marbles, people ran every which way, including me. We were blessed that no one was hit.

* * *

Countless hours of my youth were spent practicing my jump shot. But I think I spent even more time trying to write. Not fiction or poetry but political writing. My workstation was a linoleum-topped table in my grandma's kitchen. I'd write over the family chatter, trying to mirror my Aunt Diane's ability to shut out all the noise, usually while my Grandma Dorothy cooked. Sometimes my political writing took priority over my schoolwork. I'd get lost in it, in a zone.

My white notebook paper would fill up with pressing ideas on how redlining needed to be abolished, or how it wasn't fair that Black people were paid less than white people, or why the Vietnam War should end. Word by word, I tried to shape my thoughts into appeals to politicians in Washington, DC.

My mom and aunts treated the political questions of the day seriously, and it rubbed off on me. Conversations about voter registration laws, the war in Vietnam, the "poverty draft"—the unequal impact of the draft on African Americans and the poor—public housing, school segregation in Chicago, women's rights in the workplace, and many other topics flowed during and after dinner most nights. I'd be a fly on the wall during these discussions and would leave with my nerves frayed. When they saw the worried looks across my young face, my mom and aunts, like clockwork, would say, "Write it down, Craig. Your stomach and heart know the answer. Let your mind and pen process it for you. We'll send what you come up with to Congressman So-and-So when you are finished." They didn't trust that Congress could solve all our problems, but they did believe in pressuring the system from all angles. Mostly they wanted me to feel like my voice could challenge racism, war, and injustice.

Writing letters to political representatives became second nature for me. Dozens of letters were stamped and dropped into the blue postbox on the corner of our street. A month or so later, I'd usually get an official form letter reply from whichever congressman I had written. Sure, it was just a form letter, but there was sense of accomplishment and validation that came from the thick paper with the official government seals that held my name. My hat was in the ring, and it made me feel proud. The world may have been full of cruelty and injustice, but at least I was doing my part to improve it.

CHAPTER 3

PLAYING THE LOTTO

Kids in my neighborhood played sports with an intensity that people who have the means to pay for college, or who have never been exposed to racism, can't understand. For us it was either get that scholarship or take the night shift at the Ford plant. And after the Ford plant closed down, it was sports or the streets.

Some people have come up with far-fetched racist explanations for Black athletes' success. Jimmy the Greek, at one time a famous commentator for CBS Sports, was fired for saying there were so many Black professional athletes because we had an extra muscle in our leg. Believe me, it's not any kind of extra muscle. The main reason there are so many Black pro athletes is that we have been limited in our options. For the vast majority of us, playing sports was like growing up depending on a lotto ticket. It might have been a snowball's chance in hell, but at least it's a chance.

It was because of this dynamic that, after my freshman year, I transferred from Bloom High School to Rich East High School.

Bloom was the school that my entire family had attended, the school the rest of the kids from the east side of town went to. It was mostly Black. Rich East was mostly white. My family hoped to give my Aunt Jeri and me a better chance at life by sending us to Rich East, the school with more resources: better-paid teachers, guidance counselors, smaller classrooms, textbooks that weren't decades out of date. Yet I protested. Raymond McCoy and I were lighting things up at Bloom. I was averaging twenty points a game and he was already beginning to receive letters from schools like UCLA and North Carolina as a freshman. The two of us would be unstoppable by senior year. Bloom also taught a Black History class sophomore year—Black History!—the class I was most interested in. My family wouldn't listen. They were determined to transfer me to the better school.

Heartbroken after the transfer, I was now one of forty Black kids at East, in a school with a student body of 1,500. I protested by refusing to play basketball—or any sport. I turned inward and stopped talking to most people, which was a shock for my friends, because I was a talker. All I could think about was what could have been if I'd stayed at Bloom with my friends.

Then there was the racism.

On Dr. King Day—which wasn't yet a federal holiday, but a day we were well aware of—that first year, all forty of us walked into school to find the words "nigger" and "coon" scrawled on our lockers. Racism had been an abstract idea to me before I transferred to Rich East. These young white racists who hid in the shadows at East made it real. I say "shadows" because we'd find the graffiti, and we'd hear the taunts echoing from a distance down the hall, but none of these racists ever had the courage to say anything to my face. Up until that point the political actions that I participated in had been equated with fun, an excuse to take a day off from school or hang out with the neighborhood kids and play sports while the grownups held their meetings. Now I began to feel the racism in my gut, like my family did, and I understood it on a different level.

Retired from sanctioned high school sports, I kept my nose in the books and earned good grades. But I missed basketball something fierce, and it was hard to pretend otherwise. One day in late fall, as I was walking down the stairs at Rich East to head home, I bumped into Coach Ricky Bell. He was my granddad's friend.

"Hey, Coach, what's up with you?" I said.

"Do you even know what I coach, Hodge? I'm the assistant varsity basketball coach. You didn't know that?"

"Nah, sorry, Coach."

"I haven't seen you in the gym. You plan on playing this year, right?"

"Probably not."

"Quit it, Hodge. You know you could contribute to this team. And we could use you."

"Yeah, I'm thinkin' I wouldn't fit in too well."

After a little more back-and-forth, Coach Bell said, "Come on. Let's go for a drive." He drove me home, a few miles from the school.

We walked into the house, where Granddad was sitting at the kitchen table drinking coffee. "Hey, Bruce, what's up with Craig? He says he ain't playing basketball this year."

"What? That's the first I'm hearing that. Craig, you're not playing ball?"

"Nah. I'm gonna focus on the books, Granddad."

"Craig, you're gonna need to find time for your athletics. . . . It's not up for debate. You hear me?"

Remember, it was sports or the factory for most of us. Yes, my granddad thought Rich East could provide us with more opportunity because it had better academic resources than Bloom, but he also knew we didn't have the luxury of throwing away chances. He saw that I had the skills to make it to the next level and possibly have college paid for. Working for the park district, Granddad saw hundreds of kids who would have given anything to have half the athletic potential I had. He was also living through me, on some level, the way parents and other family members live through their kids when their own opportunities were cut short. It wasn't just about me—it was about him, too.

Arguing with Granddad wasn't something I did, so I laced up my black low-top Converse and went back to the court. I scored twenty-five points in my first game with the sophomore East team. A giant part of me wasn't just thrilled but also relieved to be back. I hadn't known how much basketball meant to me until I almost walked away from it. In that evening's games, the sophomore team played first, then varsity. Coach Fisher, the head coach of the varsity team, handed me a uniform right then and there, after he saw what I did on the court with the sophomores. Then I sat—all game. I listened to the crowd chant and watched East build up a good lead as my butt got sore. Coach Fisher finally put me in with just five minutes to go, and I scored fourteen points. I didn't miss.

My Uncle Bruce went up to Coach Fisher after the game and said, "If you're going to play Craig with the varsity, then play him with the varsity. He should be starting. If not, keep him with the sophomores." The staff took back my varsity uniform that night. I loved my Uncle Bruce, but on this occasion I wished he'd kept his mouth shut. I would have happily worked my way onto the starting varsity lineup, but my uncle was trying to jump the line. He gambled with my place and lost. Like my granddad, Uncle Bruce was probably living through me in some ways, hoping I could fulfill his lost potential.

Kids from all backgrounds experience this kind of pressure, but Black kids feel it on a profound level. Black kids who show even the slightest chance of redeeming the lost dreams of the previous generation, either for their family or for an entire community, are zeroed in on. Intense pressure is placed on these kids. Sometimes the feelings of the child are overlooked in favor of thoughts of what the kid could become in the future. So the kids, if they want the attention and adulation, have to shut down certain parts of themselves and live entirely for a projected idea of themselves. My family stressed balance, and they clearly loved me for who I was, not who they wanted me to be, but I still felt the pressure. I didn't always admit it, but it was there. Other kids have it a lot worse, though. What happens when a college or the NBA doesn't come knocking? In a certain sense the child stops existing. An emptiness sets in. They become a ghost, animated only by the memories of who they were, and they forfeit the person they could become.

✱ ✱ ✱

I was getting a lot of colleges sniffing around me—and what a time to be on the recruitment radar. The late '70s and early '80s were the Wild West of college recruiting. Recruiters arrived in neighborhoods like Chicago Heights with fists full of dollars, car keys, clothing, furniture, and unlimited restaurant tabs in the hopes of buying up as much talent as they could get their hands on.

Texas A&M sent a recruiter named Norm Ruther to Chicago Heights with a single order: bring Raymond McCoy back to Texas or don't bother coming home. Raymond was only a freshman at the time, so Norm bunkered in. Living in a raggedy apartment complex, wearing the same old tracksuit day after day, Norm turned up time and again at King courts or at Bloom High, stoically watching Raymond. After each scrimmage or game we'd see Norm lingering, ready to lay out cash like a long-lost creepy rich uncle. "Hodge, you want to go grab a few filet mignons? It's on me," Raymond would say after a pickup game.

Raymond was always flush, and his friends benefited from his good fortune even beyond nice dinners. Raymond would tell Norm, "Hey, my friends could use a few bucks," and Norm would dive into his pocket without thinking about it and hand us each a five. As Raymond's game improved, he became bolder. "Come on, Norm, now what are we gonna buy with five bucks each?" So Norm would give us ten. A streak of guilt, like I was doing something I wasn't supposed to, ran through me every time I accepted the money. But I thought, *Hey, Raymond is getting a lot more than I am, and I'm nearly as good as Raymond.* So I suppressed the doubt. When you have no paper in your pocket, it's always easy to justify.

In Chicago Heights, most people were lucky to have three square meals or were working their lives away on a night shift, so, in our eyes, these recruiters didn't just come with money: they came with the promise of freedom, new experiences, and opportunity. That placed a lot of pressure on Raymond, even if he didn't outwardly express it. If someone wasn't getting enough playing time, they'd go to Raymond and ask him to talk to the coaches on their behalf. I'm sure adults looking for handouts approached him for money as well. Raymond was an easygoing guy, who—as a teenager—was now cast in the role of rainmaker. The whole town watched Raymond and rooted for their version of him. For the most part he played the role. Raymond had the coaches and the money people from the universities wrapped around his finger. He could pull strings whenever he wanted.

When Raymond graduated high school he was the #1-ranked guard in Illinois. A guy you might have heard of named Isiah Thomas, over at St. Joe, was #2. At the time, the McDonald's All-Americans included players like Dominique Wilkins, James Worthy, Byron Scott, John Paxson. They wouldn't play a summer league game without getting paid. Five hundred dollars per game (that's 1970s dollars) was about the going rate. Not one of those players could be considered an amateur by the time they entered college. The money came from boosters who wanted to see their alma mater win and profit off the talent of these kids. Everyone within arm's reach of these star players tried to get their piece.

So it didn't come as much of a surprise when Raymond passed over Texas A&M. A booster from San Francisco swooped in at the eleventh hour and paid Raymond's brother a huge chunk of change— probably not as much as poor old Norm had shelled out all those years—to convince Ray to go to the University of San Francisco. Raymond regretted the decision almost immediately. "With that decision, I just lost something," he said. "I lost a lot of competitiveness that night because I didn't feel comfortable."[3] Raymond arrived at the University of San Francisco and found the basketball program on probation for (...*drum roll*...) recruiting violations. So Raymond hardly played his freshman year. He transferred to DePaul and was forced to sit out another full season because of transfer rules.[4]

When Raymond finally had his chance, he couldn't recapture the fire that made him and started only five games. As of his senior year at DePaul, Raymond was playing only five minutes a game. The *Chicago Tribune* published an article on Ray and his career in 1993. Ray was coaching eighth-grade basketball, whereas Isiah Thomas was still playing for the Detroit Pistons. As Raymond told the *Chicago Tribune*:

> From my sophomore year on, college was something I became depressed about. I couldn't come to grips with being in basketball and not being successful as I always had been. Everywhere I'd go, people asked why I was not playing. Even now they still see you as a person who still should be playing. "Why didn't you play?" I couldn't answer it.

The article never mentioned the finances involved in the recruiting process, which left a gaping hole in the story. Money was at the heart of all that happened to Ray as a basketball player—money and the artificial, fleeting support that came (and went) from those who wanted a cut of his action.

Colleges began reaching out to me my junior year. Nothing compared to Raymond, but the University of Wyoming, the first big school to show interest, wanted me bad. They invited me out for a visit. I didn't know much about the school other than it was in a state that seemed to like cowboys. After the plane touched down in Laramie, our group of recruits was greeted by a welcome party and promptly given a tour of the campus and a light lunch. Like at Rich East, the Black people on the Wyoming campus were difficult to spot. It seemed the only nonwhite people at the school were in my group, being given a tour. The assistant coach in charge of the tour announced that he had a surprise for us, later in the day.

A few hours later, he exclaimed, "You're all going snowmobiling!" The other recruits and I looked around at each other, confused but willing to go along with the plan. They started handing out pillowy brown-and-yellow snowsuits in the university's colors, and before I knew it I was in a Kawasaki, climbing the side of a mountain with a bunch of other high school students. "You know, Craig, if you sign with Wyoming I'll see to it that your family back in Chicago gets a new refrigerator and a new set of living room furniture," said a portly booster, who had tagged along on the trip, as we reached the top of the mountain.

He must own a furniture store, I thought to myself.

"But you'll have to sign with us before you go home. No pressure . . . think about it. Enjoy yourself tonight. You're going to love it here," said the booster.

I nodded my head and said OK, and we went back down the mountain.

I knew my granddad wouldn't want someone he didn't know refurbishing his house, but, standing atop that snowy mountain in the middle of nowhere, I also saw the offer as a gift to my family.

Something I'd earned. My granddad and grandma went without many comforts raising a huge family. If anyone deserved a few new appliances, they did.

A line of young, well-dressed women met us in the student lounge after we'd all cleaned up following our outdoor adventure. "Who's ready to party?!" asked one of them. We were led to a dorm room, where we started drinking, listening to music, and eventually hooking up with these young women. *I could get used to this*, I thought.

The next morning we were all asked to sign letters of intent. "I'm not ready to make any formal commitments today, but I can verbally commit if that helps you," I said. The coach asking us to sign was clearly disappointed but saw that I was resolved in my decision. "OK, Craig. We'll give you a little more time to think about it. The offer still stands—your family will be taken care of when you eventually decide that you want to be a Cowboy." I thanked him and headed to the airport.

A month or two later, the school sent coaches out to meet my family and get the letter of intent signed. As I walked toward the house after practice I could see a rental car in the driveway. A wave of fear crashed over me. I crept up to the front window of our house and saw the coaches from Wyoming talking with my granddad. I froze there for a moment. Finally I shook the ice out of my head and walked into the house, right past the coaches and my grandparents, and went down to the basement without saying a word. I knew my granddad would be furious that I'd accepted the furniture. So I hid.

Granddad walked down the stairs a few seconds later to ask what the hell I was doing.

"They promised you and Grandma all this nice stuff if I signed with them. Free furniture. I said 'yes.' Now I don't know if I want to go there anymore. I think I'd be going to Wyoming, to become a Cowboy, for the wrong reasons."

"Listen, Craig. Basketball is for you. Should you take advantage of a scholarship if they offer it to you? Yes, of course. But don't go making these big life decisions so your grandma and I can get new furniture."

My granddad had principles. He grew up thinking that nothing should be given to someone unless it was up front and open. I like to think Granddad knew I was worth more than a refrigerator. He wanted me to set my sights higher. If I wasn't going to be paid what I was worth, I shouldn't let them think anything less was OK.

CHAPTER 4

NEW HORIZONS

The summer between my sophomore and junior year, Uncle Larry said, "Up until now you have been doing everything off the dribble. Time to start working on your catch and release."

Uncle Larry spent hour after hour (after hour) passing the ball to me at all the different points on King court: the elbow, the corner, the top of the key, and back again. I must have shot a million jumpers that summer with Uncle Larry. Then there was the solo time I spent with toss-backs—where I would spin the ball out in front of me and have it come back, replicating a pass—when I was by myself. Shot after shot, day after day, I practiced in every weather condition. Taller, faster, bigger players seemed to be around every corner, but I felt like I worked harder than all of them. I had one obsession: it wasn't to make every shot. It was having the quickest release on any court I stepped on. That meant perfection—in form and follow-through.

Junior year, I finally got the chance to play against my old teammates from Bloom in the state regional finals. Bloom's blue-and-white stadium was standing room only for the cross-town rivalry. We were on the road, and we were the underdogs. This would be the first time my buddies from the east side of Chicago Heights would see me play with Rich East. The regional game was high stakes, no matter the matchup. Yet this night, the air was a little thicker than usual: the game against Bloom was about bragging rights between the mostly white versus mostly Black town rivals. Personally, I felt this was my chance to show everyone I was the most underrated player not only in town but in all of Illinois. I wanted that level of recognition from college scouts; I wanted my respect.

Right out of the gate it was me versus Fred Jones, Bloom's star shooting guard. Fred was quick, with smooth handles, and he had a gorgeous jump shot. I got right at it with Fred. It was back and forth, one on one, all night. He'd take the ball down the court and hit a jumper from the top of the key. Then I'd take the rock and do the same thing. I remember that game like it was yesterday: the orange glow of the gym lights, the creak of the hardwood, the chants from the stands, the smell of hotdogs, popcorn, and nacho cheese warming in the concession stands in the hall outside the gym. Everyone was there, especially the recruiters, the gatekeepers of our future.

I scored twenty-eight that night. We won when we were expected to lose. "Where did he come from?" "I didn't know he was that good!" My name buzzed around like the gym lights after the game. It was a turning point in my high school career. We usually went out to Barnaby's Pizza after games for our "after action reports," but I skipped the pizza, went home, and lay on top of the covers of my bed with the lights out.

Still in my street clothes, hands clasped behind my head, I stared at the Julius Erving poster that hung on my wall. The lights from the street lit a leaping Dr. J with his arms extended, legs crossed in midair, in his Sixers uniform, and he looked almost Christ-like. The shot's angle was from the floor so he seemed extra tall, like he was dunking through a basket that hung from the stadium rafters. He had an afro and the American flag hung in the background. It was a red, white, blue, and Black poster.

The future looked wide open. Basketball would bring me the college scholarship that would allow me to get the education my aunts and mom had encouraged: an education I had grown to want myself. I would be the first male in my family to graduate college. Yet I thought about playing in the pros, too, even more than college. The NBA was within my reach, and I couldn't ignore that.

All of a sudden the biggest coaches in the NCAA were at my door. "The General," Bob Knight, rang the house one night and said, "We want you at Indiana, but you'll have to cut your afro." Guess I wouldn't be going to IU. A young Rick Pitino sent me a letter asking me to play for Syracuse, where he was the assistant under Jim Boeheim. "You'll make a valuable contribution to our program," Pitino said. These coaches and others like them wanted their players to keep their mouth shut, look right in the uniform, and get good grades to stay eligible so their program could win, which is fine. However, I could sense in these letters and calls that the college game was more about the coaches' careers, disguised in language about service to the university, than about the players' careers. None of these coaches ever mentioned the next level—the NBA.

My junior year, Coach Tex Winter from Northwestern emerged from the stands to greet me after one of our games. He asked if I wanted to play for him. "I think you have what it takes to make it to the pros one day, Craig. We need to work on your fundamentals, though." We sat down and had a long chat. Coach Winter had been the head coach of the Houston Rockets before taking the position at Northwestern. He told me he preferred coaching college because there was a greater focus on team play and teaching the fundamentals of basketball.

Coach Winter mentioned the triple-post offensive system that night, a system he'd developed, and described how it would prepare me for the NBA. That system would later become famous under Coach Phil Jackson as "the triangle." Coach Winter seemed less superficial than the other college coaches. At the library the next day, I looked him up and learned that he had been NCAA Coach of the Year in 1958. His Kansas State Wildcats defeated Oscar Robertson's #2-ranked Cincinnati Bearcats to earn a spot in the Final Four. That was impressive.

From the beginning, Coach Winter encouraged me to follow my dreams. He clearly thought a lot about maximizing a player's longevity, beyond college. Even though by now I was used to brushing off recruiters and coaches, Coach Winter was harder to ignore, and he kept coming back. After the first Chicago city/suburban high school game, where I played one of the best games of the year, with thirty points and seven assists, Coach Winter approached me and said, "Hey, Craig, I am leaving Northwestern for Long Beach State. It will be a fresh start, and I want you to come with me."

"California?" I replied.

"Yes, if you play with me for four years, I promise I will get you a tryout with a pro team."

No other coach had made such a promise. Long Beach State rose to number one on my list of schools. I trusted Coach Winter. I sensed he would do right by me. I had a year to think about it, though, so I didn't rush the decision.

The first five games of my senior year I scored more than thirty points per game and led the nation in scoring. Coach Winter left for Long Beach but not before recruiting my good friend Crawford Richmond, who played for Evanston Township and was a year older than me. Crawford and I played in the same summer league games, and he regularly stopped by our house, making a point to never miss Grandma Dorothy's Sunday brunch. In the midst of my big scoring run, Crawford called me from Long Beach State to help with Coach Winter's pitch. "Mom has been sending me your clippings, Hodge. I've been showing them to Coach Winter. He really wants you to come to Long Beach State to play for him," Crawford said.

Crawford's opinion meant a lot to me. We had a lot in common: we both cared about Black history, and we were probably the only two teenagers in the Chicago area who knew about the history of Evanston, Illinois. My great-uncle Edward Hodges, who loved to brew his own beer and talk history too, lived only two blocks from Crawford. "Ah, you two know the history of the Crawford family, don't you?" he asked us one day.

"Nope," we replied.

Uncle Edward proceeded to tell us how and why nearly every African American living in Evanston, Illinois, has ties to Abbeville, South Carolina.

According to Uncle Edward, a man by the name of Anthony Crawford was one of the wealthiest Black men living in Abbeville, South Carolina, in the early years of the twentieth century. Anthony Crawford was a successful farmer whose net worth was estimated to be close to $30,000—a ridiculous fortune for the times. A father of thirteen children, Crawford built a school on his five-hundred-acre property for his kids and the local Black kids who were shut out of white schools. Crawford did so well for himself that he often loaned white folks money for their own crops. On the morning of October 21, 1916, he walked into W. D. Barksdale's store to sell cottonseed. The going rate was 90 cents a bushel for the seed, and Barksdale low-balled Crawford by offering him 85 cents a bushel. Crawford said he could do better elsewhere, and Barksdale called him a liar. Crawford cursed at Barksdale and left the store.

Despite being one of the wealthiest members of the town, Crawford had crossed a line. Barksdale, a white man, followed him out of the store, and the two men began arguing on the street. The town sheriff swept in and arrested Crawford for yelling and cussing at Barksdale. An angry white mob gathered later at the prison. Crawford paid his bail and was released out the side entrance of the jail. As Crawford walked away, the crowd followed him and began throwing rocks. Crawford ran and took refuge in a nearby cotton mill, but McKinney Cann, the leader of the mob, caught up with him. Crawford grabbed a hammer and hit McKinney in the head. The crowd raged, but the sheriff persuaded the mob to back off, and Crawford was arrested again. This time the mob overran the jail, dragged Crawford into the streets and beat him until he was unconscious. The mob revived Crawford and then beat him again and again.

Finally, someone thought it would be a good idea to tie Anthony Crawford, the man who built a school for all the local Black kids to attend for free, to a horse-drawn buggy. Crawford's body bounced down the street behind the buggy, which made a circuit in front of every Black home in town, coursing through the streets for the remainder of the day. As the sun set someone grabbed a noose and strung Crawford over a tree branch, and then they opened fire. Crawford's body took between two hundred and four hundred bullets that night, according to Uncle Edward. His body was taken away, and to this day no one knows the location of Crawford's grave.

After the lynching, all the Black businesses in town were torched and shut down by the still-seething lynch mob. The Crawfords and nearly every other Black family in Abbeville, including Ralph Ellison Sr., the famous novelist's father, were run out of town. There was a mass migration from Abbeville to, of all places, Evanston, Illinois.

Stories like this have haunted Crawford Richmond and me our entire lives. But they also built trust between us. If he was telling me to go to Long Beach State, that had serious weight with me. Sure enough, Crawford continued to call throughout the year.

"Coach wants you on the team bad, Hodge. . . . He understands the game. . . . He'll work you hard, but you'll know a lot about basketball by the time you graduate. Plus, he gives us space. The girls aren't too bad either . . . and it's sunny every day."

Crawford was convincing. Coach Winter had the expertise I was looking for, and he emanated a positive vibe. The thought of going to school with California girls was appealing to me, too. Finally, at the end of my junior year, I called up Coach Winter and accepted his scholarship offer.

My senior year at Rich East, after the first five games of the season, Coach Fisher told me to pass more. My average dropped to twenty points a game (I'd finish the season averaging nineteen). At first I was disappointed. I knew I could score every time I touched the ball. But Coach Fisher was trying to teach me how to play as part of a team at both ends of the court. Quite a few players could take over a game; however, few knew how to pull the reins back and get the ball in the hands of an open player under the basket, or commit to defense in the critical moment of a game. There is more to basketball than scoring, and sometimes it's hard for high school players to see that—particularly players who are trying to be noticed by college coaches. It was difficult for me at first, but Coach was preparing me for the next level. He was preparing himself for the next level, too.

Coach Steve Fisher was later the head coach of the University of Michigan. He took over the head spot during the final week of the 1989 season, after Bill Frieder accepted a job at Arizona State. Athletic Director Bo Schembechler dismissed him on the spot, famously saying that only a "Michigan man" should coach Michigan. Despite the turmoil, Coach Fisher led the Wolverines to the NCAA championship that year, with a little help from star players Glen Rice and Rumeal Robinson. Fisher was also the coach of what without question was the most famous college team never to win a title, Michigan's Fab Five of Chris Webber, Jalen Rose, Ray Jackson, Jimmy King, and Juwan Howard. They made the NCAA finals in 1992 and 1993, but that's as far as they got.

Raymond McCoy and I were named co-Players of the Year in the south Chicago suburbs that year. When I went down to Champaign to play in the all-state game, many of the reporters and recruiters seemed surprised to learn I was Black. "Your scouting reports made us think you were white because you shoot like a white kid," I heard from one recruiter. I guess that was supposed to mean I didn't showboat. But I paid it no mind. After the season ended, things were looking up. My family was proud of me. So I did my best to enjoy the last months of high school.

I was confident in my own skin as an African American, which was rare at Rich East. To me it seemed like the other thirty-nine Black kids at the school tried to fit in by acting white. I acted like myself, and this impressed the ladies. Growing up with so many women in my house, I felt comfortable around the opposite sex. I began dating a young woman named Donna, my first girlfriend, the spring of my senior year. When I wasn't hooping I was chilling with Donna. She was tall, with long dark hair, and was white. As much as I was aware of racism, I saw each person, regardless of their color, as an individual with their own story. If you were white and cool then you were good with me.

And Donna was cool. We planned on going to the prom, but in the end decided against it because Donna was scared we would be ridiculed and possibly attacked for race mixing. I was less concerned about it, but I imagine Donna wanted to protect her reputation. So we drove around that night in secret. We parked in a lot by my house and began making out, thinking we were alone. A few minutes later, my car took multiple blows from a bombardment of heavy rocks. I stepped out to confront the shadowy perpetrators. The rocks stopped flying and the cowards ran.

CHAPTER 5

HEADING WEST

Growing up, my team was UCLA. They had Lew Alcindor and Bill Walton and were coached by the legendary John Wooden. Between 1964 and 1975 Wooden led the Bruins to ten NCAA championships. "Success is never final, failure is never fatal. It's courage that counts" has always been my favorite of his many axioms. In high school, when I thought of California, I thought of the Bruins.

When Coach Winter picked me up at the airport in late July before my freshman year, it was my first time in California. He knew I idolized UCLA, so rather than taking me to the Long Beach dorms, he drove to the UCLA campus in Westwood.

"What are we doing here, Coach?"

"I want you to look around. I want you to see that the place actually exists. It is important that UCLA is not some mythical school for you, Craig."

We walked into the famous Pauley Pavilion. The stadium felt dark as we entered from the bright midday Southern California sun. I looked up into the rafters. Ten national championship banners floated above the thousands of empty seats like fluttering blue-and-gold apparitions. We stood before the Mecca of college basketball.

"OK, Craig, you've been to UCLA. Here it is. Let's go," Coach said, matter-of-factly, shaking me out of my astonishment. He knew young people in particular had a way of building things up in their minds, and he sought to demystify UCLA. Not that it wasn't a great school, but we had our own business to take care of. He wanted me focused, confident in my skills, and confident in *my* school. Although I have to admit, we left UCLA and I was still as impressed as ever. That was one of the few mental exercises Coach put me through that didn't work.

The first day of practice Coach Winter said, "Anything that you have ever learned about basketball . . . well, forget it." He dragged out a ladder and grabbed two basketballs. Then he climbed above the rim and dropped both balls through the rim with ease. "The hoop is bigger than you thought. Isn't it? While you are playing for me we will break this game down into its smallest working parts. We'll put the game under a microscope, and you will see that basketball is about overcoming illusions. The most important illusion that needs to be overcome is that there are teams out there that are better than us. I have confidence that this team can do great things. My job is to make you believe it as well. Let's get to work."

Coach began teaching us the triple-post offense, also known as the triangle, almost immediately. The triangle offense is all about movement and spacing. The court is broken up into manageable sections with players always equally distributed. The spacing allows for the team to play on the strengths of its players, and lets the strengths of other teams work against them. If your team has a slasher, like Michael Jordan or Scottie Pippen, you will create opportunities for them. And the shooters will find open shots because of the effective spacing.

The triangle can also be seen as a counterpunch system. When a defense takes away a position on the court or overplays your strongest offensive player, something else opens up. You don't fight pressure in the triangle. It's the tai chi of basketball systems: all about balance, working with your opponent rather than against them. There is no way to defend against the triangle when it's properly executed. When you put a great player into the offense the team rises to their highest potential. The great players can handle the added pressure of operating inside such a system and not just playing one on one, which gives the team even more options on the court.

There is a reason why Hall of Fame coaches revere Tex Winter, and even at eighteen, I knew that if you were serious about basketball, you were serious about listening to this man. Coach gave names to every action on the court. It wasn't just stopping; it was a "one-count stride stop." A jump stop became a "two-foot jump shot to triple threat." Everything Coach did, he did for a reason. He was a thinking player's coach.

Some players, particularly the upper-classmen, didn't like Winter. They were used to playing for a coach who was less concerned with fundamentals, a coach famous for his "run-and-gun" offense, who scrimmaged his teams most practices, with whom you could get away with missing a practice or two: that coach was Jerry Tarkanian. If you know hoops, you know that there probably could not be two more different people either in terms of their game plans or temperaments than Jerry "The Shark" Tarkanian and Tex Winter.

Coach Tark had recruited most of our seniors while he was at Long Beach State from 1968 to 1973. He would go on to win a national championship at his next job, at University of Nevada–Las Vegas, with Larry Johnson, Greg Anthony, and Stacey Augmon in 1990, so I would never say Tarkanian didn't know what he was doing. He simply had a different approach to the game—an approach that fans loved and some would say revolutionized college basketball. I have nothing but love for Coach Tarkanian, but the divided loyalties on our team were real.

As a freshman, I was in the starting lineup. It was the first time a freshman guard had started at Long Beach State. I'd like to say I earned it through practice, but the truth is that the previous guard became academically ineligible. That had rarely happened under Tark. With Tex, there was a new sheriff in town. It also helped me in Coach's eyes that my studies were always on point. Before I left for college, my Aunt Diane gave me advice: "Always read two chapters ahead of the syllabus. That way you know what the professor is talking about before the lesson begins." Following Aunt Diane's advice, I never had a problem with academics.

On the court, Long Beach State went from relative obscurity to being ranked number nine in the nation. We had Ricky Williams, who went on to play for the Jazz; Francois Wise, who was drafted by the Washington Bullets; Craig Dykema, who played for the Phoenix Suns; Michael Wiley, the six-foot-nine power forward who played for the Spurs. Wiley only wore size twelve sneakers despite his size, so he tripped a lot.

I hit the first jumper I took in a college game and never looked back. By my sophomore year, I'd set the Long Beach assist record, mostly passing to Wiley, who jumped over people in those tiny shoes. We began playing powerhouse teams like Duke and North Carolina, and we caught them off guard more than once with our basketball know-how and discipline on the court, thanks to the tutelage of Coach Winter.

Coach was all about theory, but he didn't take himself too seriously either. He was light-hearted. He didn't impose crazy restrictions on us, so we never felt the need to rebel. He trusted his team; he saw his players as human beings first, and we responded to that. I'll never forget what he said after one Friday evening practice: "I can't tell you what to do at night. I will say that you can't hang out with the owls and expect to soar with the eagles."

During my sophomore year, we were on an endless and exhausting three-week road trip through the Midwest. We endured an unnatural amount of time freezing our behinds off on a rickety old school bus with a heater that sighed more than it blew. We were spent and wanted to go home. One of the final games of the trip was in Milwaukee against Marquette, and we were down big at the half. Coach Winter strolled into the locker room and found many of us laughing. All we were thinking about was how we would soon be back in the California sun with our honeys.

Standing in front of a large green chalkboard, Coach grabbed the chalk. We quieted down. "Y'all are expecting me to draw up a play right now, aren't ya? Maybe we'll talk about Marquette's defense and how they're killing us on the boards tonight? Is that what y'all are thinking?" he asked, unusually upbeat in light of the half-time deficit. "We'll be discussing something else, and I don't want it leaving this room. Y'all ready?" We nodded somewhat eagerly.

Slowly he wrote M-A-R-I-J-U-A-N-A, in capital letters, and then sharply underlined it. "*Mar-e-joo-wanna*," he said. "I'm hearing from reliable sources that we have a team full of mar-e-joo-wanna users," Coach drawled in his Texas panhandle accent. "Y'all see, I studied mar-e-joo-wanna. Ya know what mar-e-joo-wanna does?"

He paused. We squirmed in our chairs. "It puts you in a state of *euphoria*. What happens to your brain when you are in euphoria?" he continued calmly. We were silent. "I'll tell y'all, because *I* studied mar-e-joo-wanna," he repeated. "All is good with the world. Am I right?" A few heads nodded. "Well, I'll tell ya something, gentlemen, things are not good right now. Anybody who looks up at the scoreboard with decent vision can tell you that."

Coach looked at Kevin Tye, the seven-foot white surfer who was our center. "They tell me you're the ringleader, big man." Tye stared blankly at Coach.

I dropped my head, as did most of the team. Now he was getting specific. Coach looked at me next. "Craig, why're you looking at your shoes? You don't like me talking about your boy, do you?"

He knew I was Kevin's biggest customer. Busted. Our basketball careers were over. The paranoia really set in. "OK. End of discussion. Get out there and start warming up." I played the rest of the game shaking in my shoes, but I scored twenty-three points that half, a personal record. I can't say that marijuana use stopped entirely, but many of us cut back dramatically, at least before games and practices, after that halftime chat.

I enjoyed my education just as much as I enjoyed basketball. Growing up under the influence of my aunts and mom, I knew Black Studies was my calling. Long Beach State had one of the first Black Studies departments in the nation, and in the late '70s the subject was still in its infancy. Simply attending Black Studies classes was a revolutionary act in many ways. I had a professor at Long Beach State who became something of a legend as the man who created Kwanzaa and one of the key organizers of the 1995 Million Man March, professor Maulana "Ron" Karenga. Professor Karenga, a bald, barrel-chested man, connected study and struggle for me in a way no one else had.

Dr. Karenga explained the ebbs and flows in the Black liberation movement throughout US history, from slave uprisings to the voter registration marches down South and the rebellions in Watts and Detroit in the 1960s, and helped me understand that different historical moments require different tactics in the struggle. He'd draw a direct connection between police violence and unfair housing policies, or the war in Vietnam and poverty. He taught me that we couldn't simply react to injustice. We have to anticipate that injustice will be inflicted on the Black community. We have to build organizations that plan actions.

All of this had vivid context for me, newly transplanted to California. Less than a decade before my freshman year, in 1968, J. Edgar Hoover, director of the FBI, had declared the Black Panther Party (BPP) "the greatest threat to the internal security of the United States." In no uncertain terms, this was a directive to wipe them out. BPP headquarters were up in Oakland, but the systematic assassination of BPP members by the US government began in Long Beach. In December 1968, Frank "Franco" Diggs, a key member of the Southern California BPP chapter, was taken out in an alley just a little ways from Long Beach State. Among folks in Long Beach, it's taken as an article of faith that the FBI was involved. Franco's murder was the first of many.

A month later, in January 1969, the brilliant Alprentice "Bunchy" Carter and John Huggins were killed on the UCLA campus. Huggins and Carter were also founding members of the Southern California BPP chapter. They were shot and killed in a UCLA classroom during a meeting to discuss the creation of the first Black Studies program at the school. Dr. Karenga was a student at UCLA when this all went down.

The Panthers were a radical group, absolutely. The word "radical" comes from the Latin word for "root." They were trying to get at the root causes of racism in the United States, which meant studying Black history, understanding the political economy of racism, and fighting back. Self-education, self-reliance, and resistance, principles America was allegedly founded on, right? Yes, the Black Panthers carried weapons—one of the BPP's founding missions was the defense of the Black community against police brutality. The BPP's full name was the Black Panther Party for Self-Defense. As Malcolm X put it: "If we could bring about recognition and respect of our people by peaceful means, well and good. Everybody would like to reach his objectives peacefully. But I'm also a realist. The only people in this country who are asked to be nonviolent are Black people." Personally, I think violence is no answer, but I understand why the BPP armed its members.

Professor Karenga made the connection between the destruction of the BPP and the LAPD's Special Weapons and Tactics Team (SWAT) and the FBI's counterintelligence program (COINTELPRO) long before it became common knowledge. He spoke about Chicago BPP chairman Fred Hampton, who was regarded as the next great Black leader and was murdered in his bed in 1969; he talked about Franco Diggs, Huggins, and Carter; Malcolm X; and the hidden history of Martin Luther King Jr.'s radical leanings. A founder of the Us organization, viewed by some as a rival group, Professor Karenga never spoke ill of the BPP, despite the FBI's calculated efforts to pit the groups against one another. Whenever I hear a white person or even some Black people get up and talk about how the Black community needs better leadership, I go right back to what I learned in Professor Karenga's class. The US government took out an entire generation of our leadership.

My studies collided with my personal life on June 2, 1981. Ron Settles was a running back at Long Beach State and a friend of mine. We were both seniors. Ron was gearing up for a tryout with the Dallas Cowboys when the Signal Hill Police Department arrested him on June 1 for a minor speeding violation. The next morning he was found savagely beaten and hanging in his jail cell. The police ruled the death a suicide. Signal Hill, like most of the police departments in Southern California, had a reputation for being racist and violent.

Outraged by Ron's death, I helped organize a huge march up to the police station from campus. It was a three-mile walk. The riot police and SWAT were out in full force. We were scared. But we marched anyway. There was deep anger and power in the chants of the marchers. If Ron Settles could be killed by the police for no reason other than the color of his skin, then we all could. The march was multiracial, but at its fore were the Black students: this had been a lynching, something we understood all too well.

No officer was charged in the case. The papers dug up a story that Settles had written in high school, about a Black superhero who was shot but didn't die. The superhero was then hanged in a jail cell and survived. They presented this as some kind of proof that Settles took his own life. How he managed to beat himself, before the hanging, went unexplained.

We tried to memorialize Settles by wearing patches on our jerseys, but Perry Moore, the athletic director, said no. I took that to mean the athletic director at Long Beach cared more about the image of the school than the safety of his players.

I was an academic All-American my last two years at Long Beach and an NCAA Division I All-American my senior year. I achieved a lot in college, on the court and off, but what I learned from Dr. Karenga would prove the most valuable. The importance of organizing, raising my own political consciousness, and the need to challenge institutional racism took on an even greater urgency in me after the lynching of Ron Settles.

CHAPTER 6

REPRESENTING

Chicago, not California. That is where Coach Winter suggested I stay the summer after graduation. I flew back home to practice with my longtime friends Banks, Stan, Monte, Perk, Eddie, Freddie, and Raymond in Chicago Heights. We played every single day on the King courts. The summer was sweltering, with the sweat pouring off me in countless games, but I found myself in the best shape of my life. We didn't call fouls. Shooting while being roughed up is customary in the NBA. I'd heard enough guys mention this that I was determined to have tough skin by the time I had my shot.

Chicago was also the location of the NBA pre-draft training camp. Senior year of high school, Coach had said that if I stayed with him at Long Beach for four years, he'd get me a tryout with an NBA team. He kept his word, and I was a first alternate for the pre-draft camp. No one likes being an alternate, but I sensed a strong probability that I'd be called up. My college statistics gave me confidence. I'd averaged 17.5 points and 4 assists per game, and had a Long Beach record of 2 steals per game. I'd broken Long Beach State's all-time assist record with 437, and I'd scored 1,400 total points in those four years. I knew I could play with anyone at that pre-draft camp.

As luck would have it, Dwight Anderson from the University of Southern California missed check-in. On a Friday morning, Coach called me at home and asked, "How fast can you be at the Hyatt Regency?" Replying would've wasted too much time. I slammed the phone down and raced over to the hotel.

I walked on the court for a full scrimmage that evening. I hit every jumper and most of my baskets didn't touch the rim. I looked up and saw legends like Jerry West and Red Auerbach taking notes from the stands, and faintly heard, "Who's that? Where'd he come from?" I could feel a shift. The next day, Saturday, I was even better than the day before. I continued to sense eyes on me. Following the camp I was calm and confident. I could truly say that I gave it my all.

The night of the 1982 NBA draft all my aunts, uncles, cousins, friends, neighbors, and neighbors' kids packed into our house. It was standing room only—all the people who'd helped get me to this point, all those closest to me, were jammed into the living room trying to glimpse the Zenith color TV. Back then they only televised the first two rounds. The living room turned silent and somber when my name wasn't called. I thanked everyone and tried to sound hopeful, saying, "Not a problem. I'll become a free agent. It will all turn out good." The TV clicked off. Some people started to shuffle out of the house.

Minutes later, I received a call from Paul Silas of the San Diego Clippers. Paul was one of the NBA's first Black coaches. I was the second player picked in the third round, and the forty-eighth player overall. "Time to go to work!" leapt from my mouth. The room and the front yard erupted in cheers. The best game I'd played at Long Beach had been at San Diego State, where the Clippers played. I was thirteen for thirteen, with twenty-six points. It felt like fate— God's blessing.

The happiest person that night was my granddad, who'd always wanted to play professional baseball. Even in his older age he threw a baseball harder than anyone I knew. "I can die and go to heaven now, Craig," he said with a slight crack in his voice. My friends said, "Let's go, Craig. We've got to get you ready." We grabbed a basketball and jogged over to King courts.

Before I knew it I was on a plane to sunny Los Angeles for the LA summer pro camp, where I began running with the Clippers' other draft picks, like Fred Slaughter, who had played for UCLA. Four of the Clippers' draft picks were from Chicago: Terry Cummings, who'd played for DePaul; myself; Darius Clemons, who went to Loyola University in Chicago; and Eddie Hughes, who was picked in the seventh round. Eddie played for Colorado State and was from the Austin neighborhood in Chicago. He was only five-ten and 165 pounds, but he was quick as lightning. Eddie and I were essentially vying for the same spot.

The Clippers had greats like Randy Smith, Tom Chambers, and a bonafide legend in the recently acquired Bill Walton. I'd finally get to see how my skills matched up with the best in the world.

We ran the screen-and-roll offense at the camp. I missed Coach Winter's triple-post offense, but I improved with each scrimmage and practice. To be honest, I didn't know I was as good as I was. I tried to block out the fact that I could be cut at any time, and when I'd get nervous or feel my confidence waning, I'd call up memories of Arthur Ashe meditating on the tennis court. I'd repeat to myself: *Do what you've been doing for the last four years.*

I made it past the next round of cuts, and the competition continued to intensify. I was now playing against Magic Johnson, Larry Bird, and the guy whose poster I still had on my wall back home, Dr. J. I was initially in awe of these superstars, but on the court, in the heat of the game, they were humans: just flesh and blood. I tried to identify and exploit their weaknesses rather than being dazzled by their strengths, just as Coach Winter had taught me from day one, when he took me to UCLA and bluntly said, "You've seen it. Now we have work to do."

Few spectators showed up to the preseason games, but this was high-stakes ball for us. There were many guys like me who didn't want to go back to the hood. We balled like our lives depended on it. At times, dribbling and running up and down that hardwood felt like I was playing on a narrow plank that ran between two ledges; below was a fiery pit.

✳ ✳ ✳

Terry Cummings would make the club, that much was obvious. He was the Clippers' first-round pick and a power forward who could score—absolutely unstoppable on the block. My main rival, Eddie Hughes, and I were roommates in a cramped hotel room near the stadium. I insisted on taking the bed farthest from the door because I didn't want easy access to the exit. I wasn't going home.

In the final preseason game, we were down fifteen points when Coach Silas put Eddie and me in at the same time. We both seemed to be overtaken by the mysterious "zone" that athletes can sometimes experience. Each trip down the court, one of us would cause a turnover or force a bad shot, and then we'd dribble down to our end and score with ease. Only about five hundred people were in the stadium for that game, but a do-or-die energy radiated off our bodies that night.

Eddie and I brought the team back to win, and afterward we shook hands. We had nothing but respect for each other—but one of us had to go. We were back in the hotel when the phone rang. I answered it. . . . Coach Silas asked to speak to Eddie. I looked at him, and his head dropped. My heart went out to him, but I had never been happier. I signed an unguaranteed contract until Christmas. If I made it to Christmas without being cut I'd make the league minimum of

$40,000 (about $115,000 in 2015 dollars) for three years. It felt like a dream.

I earned that spot on the Clippers because Paul Silas could see that I understood the fundamentals of basketball and could also shoot the lights out. Like Coach Winter, Paul was a smart coach who wouldn't jump all over me if I screwed up. He knew everything was a lesson if looked at the right way. I broke into the starting lineup a third of the way through my rookie season and passed the Christmas finish line I had won the lotto.

My first check arrived on a Saturday. I tore open an envelope with the Clippers logo on it and saw a $2,500 check made out to Craig Hodges. I felt like a grown man for the first time. There was so much pride wrapped up in that moment. I immediately thought of sending flowers to my mom, grandma, and aunts. This was their day as much as it was mine. I wanted to pay them back, even in a small way, for a lifetime of love and support.

Then I noticed there was something missing from the check: a signature. My heart sort of sank, but I figured it was a mistake. Later that day at practice, I asked around, and none of the other players' checks had been signed, either. What kind of owner would commit such an oversight and make his players feel so disrespected? I quickly found out. The owner of the San Diego Clippers was none other than Mr. Donald Sterling.

Three decades later, Sterling would be run out of the NBA for being a racist, but for the time being we had to live with him. He claimed that not signing our checks was a mistake. Apparently this "mistake" happened a lot. Don was greedy like that; we figured he wanted to earn as much interest on his money as possible. By the time our checks were signed it would be a few days later—sometimes a week. When you do that a few times, multiplied by all the members on the team, that added up to a lot of extra interest for good ol' Don. So, on a day that should have been momentous and liberating for me,

I was mostly embarrassed to learn that I wasn't as free as I thought I was.

Soon after this first check-cashing issue with Don, I was practicing my jumper before a game when I heard an unusually deep voice call out, "Hey, Rook, come shag my balls." It was Bill Walton. He had entered the stadium late and was shooting at the opposite end of the court. I ignored him. Bill had won one NBA title with the Portland Trail Blazers, was a finals and regular-season MVP, and had been a three-time college player of the year, with two national championships under John Wooden at UCLA. As one of the greatest centers to play the game, when Bill called, people came running. In fairness, he was recovering from major knee surgery, too. But I didn't want to get in the habit of being heeled by anyone and didn't care what it cost me. It surprised him when I continued to shoot my own ball, at my end of the court, unmoved by his increasingly louder attempts. He gave up and called over Jim Brogan, a second-year player. Jim hustled over.

Later that week we were all on a plane heading to the East Coast for a long road trip. Bill was the last person to board the plane. I had the best seat because I was the first to board. I always tried to be on time. I was reading a book when I heard that same low voice say, "Hey, Rook, you're in my seat." I looked up to see this tower of a man awkwardly bending over, barely fitting his six-eleven frame inside the fuselage of the plane. I sympathized with him and his fragile knee, but I knew he'd live if he had to find another seat. I returned to my book. He repeated himself. Again, I ignored him. He knew where it was going. Once more, he turned to poor Jim Brogan and said, "Hey, Brogan, you're in my seat." Jim got up and we flew to New York.

As a Clipper, I read in the locker room, I read on the bus, I read in the gym after practice—history and religious texts, mostly. I'd ask my teammates during downtime, "What do you think about reparations? What do you think about the civil rights movement? What did you think about the day Dr. King was killed?" Paul Silas, being a Black coach, made the environment amenable to these types of questions. Paul was a silent warrior. He understood what it meant to be a strong Black man in this league. When I received a positive or open-minded response from a player, I shared what I had been reading at that moment. On a few occasions I caught Bill Walton eavesdropping on those conversations. I knew Bill was an old hippie, but I wasn't sure how he would take my enthusiasm for politics and religion. Would he rat on me to Sterling? Would he discourage others from listening to me?

Bill grabbed me in the bar at one of our hotels on that East Coast trip. I sat down and prepared for a stern lecture on how I needed to correct my attitude and show more respect to guys like him. I'd challenged Bill too many times to expect anything less. "What do you think about being the Clippers players' representative?" he asked bluntly. This wasn't the conversation I had anticipated. My eyes widened in surprise and I felt myself relax. "What would my responsibilities be?" I asked.

I'd been so concerned with making and staying on the team that I'd given little thought to our team's union. Now Walton wanted me to represent it? It seemed bizarre. Maybe it was a setup?

"Craig, management and players are different species. I'm sure you are beginning to see this by now," Bill said. I thought back to Sterling's unsigned checks. He continued, "Players and owners often have competing interests."

Bill went on for twenty minutes on the importance of players' unions—saying that unions got a bad rap in this country and that they were our only defense against the team bosses. I nodded my head in agreement.

"Craig, you have to always make sure you side with your teammates. You have to put up a united front against the owners. If you have disagreements about the direction of the club, you work that out in private." Bill was talking about the business side of the game. He knew unions were only as strong as their ability to withstand pressure from management. They could fire one person but couldn't really fire the whole team, at least not without a number of major complications.

"I think you have courage, Craig. You know how to stand up for what you believe in, all qualities that make for a good union rep." Bill saw something in me. He liked the way I played and knew I was sensitive to injustice.

I said I would do it. I started to think critically about why the owners were paid more than the players. Where would the league be without the players? Where would the *owners* be without the players? I don't think the owners could ever convince ten or twenty thousand people to buy tickets to watch them sit around a table and count money. (Besides, where would the money come from?) Yet the owners are the best compensated people in the league. They say the higher profits dished out to owners reflect risk. But tell me who risks more? The players are the people out there making it all happen, grinding it out day and night, playing through injuries. The players are the ones taking the risk.

Bill became a big brother to me, but I kept it cool around him, though. I never acted like he was one of my heroes, although he was. I didn't know it at the time, but I had become the first rookie to be named the players' representative for an NBA team.

CHAPTER 7

CARLITA

The summer before I was drafted, Ernie "Banks" Harper and I were driving down Lincoln Highway in Chicago Heights when we saw a woman standing on the side of the road, in front of a disabled green car with a steaming engine. Long-legged, with braids, and wearing a light-blue sundress, she was talking with my friend Phillip from Bloom High. "Hey, pull over," I told Banks.

We stopped in front of the car, got out, and walked over to check on the situation. The shoulder of the road was littered with beer cans and empty liquor bottles. "Hey, my man. What's up?" Banks and I directed our conversation to Phillip but were looking at this beautiful woman out of the corners of our eyes. Phillip glared, knowing our stop wasn't about him.

"Carlita, this is Hodge and Banks," he said, frowning. Carlita's car had stalled in the summer heat, and all the able-bodied men in the surrounding area were swooping in to save the day. Banks started flirting.

I interrupted in order to be the first to actually ask if I could help with the car. "You know about cars?" she asked.

"Of course I do."

Banks smirked and kept talking. Phillip continued to scowl. I kicked some broken glass away, propped up the car's hood all the way, and stared blankly at the exhausted transmission in the hot sun. I had no idea what I was looking at. I hoped that maybe God would whisper a few mechanic's secrets in my ear as an act of mercy. I heard nothing but the hissing of the engine and Banks's jabber. I loosened then tightened caps, squeezed a few hoses, and knocked on all the hard places of the engine with my knuckles.

I looked over my shoulder and saw Carlita checking me out while Banks continued. Phillip was now talking to an old man across the street. "You sure you know what you're doing over there?" Carlita asked. That's when I noticed her smile. My legs started to wobble. I was staring at Nefertiti, or at least a close relative of the Egyptian queen.

"Everything seems to be in order," I said. "This is just what happens when it gets hot. Just give it some time. It will start up eventually."

I felt like I was in a clichéd movie. Nervously, I asked if she was from the neighborhood. We talked a bit, and I found out that she knew a few of my friends.

Now Banks stood quiet, looking like a dog in the rain. "Let's go, Craig. We got places to be," he said.

"Can I have your number?" I wondered if it sounded too eager. "Sure."

I wrote it on the back of my greasy hand. Carlita hopped back in the car and turned the key in the ignition. The engine stuttered a bit and finally turned over. "The Green Monster lives," she said, waving as she drove off.

I called her up later that day. I couldn't wait.

The following Sunday Carlita picked me up for our date. I still didn't have a car. Wearing a breezy summer dress, showing off her athletic legs, sitting in the brown pleather driver's seat, she looked so fine I could barely catch my breath. Suited and booted, I was feeling fresh myself. We drove to the Nation of Islam Temple on Stony Island Avenue in Chicago. Most people take their first date to a movie, but not me; I take my first dates to hear the minister Louis Farrakhan speak.

I had learned about the Nation of Islam from Dr. Khalid Mohammad, one of my Black Studies professors at Long Beach. The name Khalid, which means "warrior," was given to him by Farrakhan. The professor would bring videos of the minister's sermons in for us to watch in class. With his gold-rimmed glasses, bright suits, and tightly waxed hair, Farrakhan and his message resonated with me on multiple levels. He spoke to my strong sense of justice and my desire to learn more about Black history, and he articulated a way forward for my people. He also fulfilled the spiritual longing I carried with me.

Because the Nation was such an emboldened group, attending one of Minister Farrakhan's services felt like an act of rebellion, a rejection of white supremacy, and an opportunity to hear a fuller range of the African American voice. Only Blacks were allowed to attend the services. People misunderstand this policy. Black people need a place they can go and be by themselves without fear or anxiety about the "white gaze." You have to be Black to understand the depths of what I mean. There was a divine calmness that accompanied the experience, despite the minister's fiery speech. It was almost like escaping to a protected island when you walked through the doors of the gold-domed temple.

When I asked Carlita to attend a service with me, I wasn't just hoping she would vibe to what the minister was all about. She had already told me, when we spoke on the phone, that she had attended the minister's services. To me, the fact that she was already a part of this scene meant she was courageous, inquisitive, interested in self-care, and probably a little too serious about life—like me.

It was starting to mist outside as we walked through the temple doors. As we entered the immaculate space, Carlita was ushered off to the female section of the temple. In the Nation, men were taught that they were the protectors of women. It was a structured world that was, in a way, the opposite of how it was outside the temple doors, where Black women were abused by a system that, in many cases, restricted them to the worst types of menial jobs—domestic labor and such.

On this particular day, the separation also allowed me to get my bearings. Sitting apart from each other, I wouldn't have to choose between holding her hand or not. Distractions were few once you were inside the temple.

∗ ∗ ∗

After the service Carlita and I went out to eat at a diner back in Chicago Heights. We each ordered a cheeseburger and fries with a Coke. I watched her as she ate. Everything she did was beautiful. We spent a few hours talking about our futures. I talked too much, going on about Black history and basketball, but she never let on that she was bored. There was a charged connection between us in that booth. It was undeniable.

"Do you want to go grab a drink somewhere?" she asked after I'd paid the bill. There was a hint of danger in her voice.

"I have to get up early to practice tomorrow."

"It's not even dark out!"

I shrugged my shoulders.

"Craig, do you worry you might be too intense about life sometimes?"

"Maybe, but I don't know any other way to be."

"I hear you. Just make sure you make time for fun, Craig," she said with a smile.

Carlita dropped me off at home and I gave her a kiss on the cheek. We dated for the rest of the summer. When I told Carlita I'd been drafted by the Clippers she responded, "You're going into the navy? To be on a ship? Why would you do such a thing?" After I shipped out, I called her every day.

Clippers attendance averaged about four thousand a game in the 1982–83 season. We finished out the year just 25–57. I made the all-rookie team, averaging 9.9 points a game, Sterling promised me a bonus if I scored ten points a game, but Don never, ever rounded up. After two seasons Paul Silas was let go, and Jim Lynam from St. Joseph University in Philadelphia was named head coach. He brought his own point guard with him, Bryan Warrick, who began starting in front of me. Bryan had only played a few seasons in the league and had a career average of four points per game. He was a good teammate but simply just wasn't as skilled as I was. I kept my mouth shut trying to hide my displeasure, playing hard during practice and making the most out of the minutes I was given. That's the thing about the NBA—you never know when it's all going to end, which kept me and a lot of players on edge.

There is an impression that players are partying nonstop on the road. I— and many of my teammates—rarely did, because most nights we were too exhausted. Teams didn't charter flights back then, we flew commercial. The alarm would go off at 5 a.m. the morning after a game, and, later that day, sometimes in a city four time zones away, we would be playing again at the highest level at 6:30 p.m. And you'd better make that early-morning flight or else you were buying your own ticket at last-minute prices, in addition to any fine the team dropped on you. On top of all that rookies were responsible for carrying the team's bags. In the early '80s you paid your dues if you wanted to play in the NBA.

∗   ∗   ∗

I flew Carlita out to be with me midway through my rookie season. The morning of March 3, 1983, I woke her up early. She threw on a pair of jeans and a T-shirt, and we drove to a chapel to get married. I had a game that night, so after the ceremony I went straight back to our apartment and took a nap—I am far from the most romantic guy in the world. Carlita seemed happy. I was happy. We'd both grown up with our fathers living outside the home, and marriage felt like it was something we needed to do in spite of our both being scared of it. We checked the box and made it official.

* * *

Carlita gave birth to our son Jibril in San Diego on February 16, 1984. She was an attentive and conscientious young mother. Jibril was a beautiful light in our home, but things started to change for the worse soon after, provoked in part by my constant traveling and Carlita's fear that I was cheating on her on the road.

Her fear was understandable. It's well known that a good number of professional athletes find sexual comfort outside of marriage in hotel rooms across the United States during road trips, but cheating on my wife is one thing I can categorically say I did not do. I was not a womanizer. Not because I was on any kind of moral high horse; I was focused on staying in the NBA. Jeopardizing my career by bringing undue stress into my life from hiding a relationship, or even a one-night stand, wasn't something I could afford.

But Carlita's suspicions only grew as I continued to travel. I assured her I wasn't a cheater, but no matter how much I insisted, she would come after me. As I sat on the couch, trying to decompress after a game or a road trip, out of nowhere she'd yell, "I know you are with other women when you are on the road, Craig. Admit it!" After a while I started to ignore her. I'd smoke a joint and just tune out the world.

Only after we were married did I learn the extent of Carlita's tumultuous childhood. The fifth of nine kids, she grew up even poorer than I did in Chicago Heights. Carlita's father beat her mother, giving her two black eyes while she was six months pregnant. Carlita didn't see her father until she was ten, and then it was through prison bars. He was on the inside for armed robbery. Her grandfather, a pastor, molested Carlita's older sisters many times before they were ten.[5] Carlita was haunted by not knowing whether her grandfather had molested her, too.

These demons followed her into our marriage. She'd blow up at me out of the blue, and not just because of the prospect of cheating. She distrusted men as a result of growing up around abuse. I can only imagine how painful it was for her, with all the trauma swirling around her mind. But where does a person draw the energy to endlessly deny false allegations and deflect volatile behavior? The accusations mounted. It was exhausting. I felt sympathy for her, but I had to live my life.

When she started to dismiss my efforts to fight for racial justice is when we began to live in entirely separate worlds. "Craig's hung up on his Black thing again," she would say, or, "Why are you living in the past with all this Black history stuff?" Our son kept us together, though. She was an excellent mother.

We didn't talk about mental health care, or at least I didn't consider it as an option. So we shut down around each other for the most part and tried to cope as best we could. Carlita was smart, and she dealt with the turmoil of her childhood by burying herself in books. Reading was her way of escaping. I loved books, too, but the books I read felt all too real sometimes. My main means of escape were basketball, my friends, and weed.

The summer of 1984, after I'd played two seasons in San Diego, word came that the Clippers were moving up to Los Angeles. LA was where Don Sterling had made his fortune in real estate as a slumlord extraordinaire. The move was most likely motivated by Sterling's envy of his friend Jerry Buss. Two years prior, Buss had purchased the LA Lakers, in part with money he'd made selling Sterling an apartment building. Buss's first year in the league, the Lakers won the 1980 NBA championship with rookie Magic Johnson and the great Kareem Abdul-Jabbar. That same year the Clippers finished the season 30–52. And things only got worse from there. The Clippers' winning percentage was .207 in the 1981–1982 season and .305 my first year with the team. My second season, Sterling purchased billboard space across the county that read "My Promise: I Will Make You Proud of the Clippers."

Carlita and I were looking for condos in Los Angeles a day before training camp when I received the call that I had been traded to the Milwaukee Bucks. It was a mega-deal: Terry Cummings—1982–1983 Rookie of the Year—Ricky Pierce, and I were traded for Marques Johnson, Junior Bridgeman, and Eddie Jordan. Marques, who averaged almost twenty points and seven rebounds a game throughout his seven-year career, was one of the best forwards in the league. Terry had been one of top five power forwards in the league as a rookie, averaging nearly twenty-three points and ten rebounds a game. The trade ended up being great for me. I'd now be on a contender.

CHAPTER 8

MILWAUKEE

I lived in a hotel room in Milwaukee for over a month, practicing with the Bucks in preseason training camp. Carlita stayed in San Diego to pack up the apartment. When she and Jibril finally arrived in Milwaukee, it was a clean start.

Milwaukee was far from cosmopolitan, and the weather was about as different from San Diego as one can imagine, but the move back to the Midwest was good for all of us. It freed Carlita from the isolation and depression that had weighed heavily on her in Southern California. She had never been close friends with the other players' wives or felt like she could call San Diego home. Many of our fights were born of her frustrations with being too far from her mom and sisters. In Milwaukee, our families were only a ninety-minute drive away.

Now our relatives could help with the babysitting and supply Carlita with the support and contact she craved. And we would require it more than ever, as Carlita became pregnant with our second son, Jamaal, during the transition. Members of both our families soon became fixtures around the hotel and, eventually, our new suburban home. Sometimes a trade to another NBA franchise can break your heart; other times it can fill it up. This was the latter. My coach was Hall of Famer and three-time Coach of the Year Don Nelson, and he was working me harder than I had ever worked before. Things felt right personally and professionally in Milwaukee— at least in the beginning.

The Milwaukee Bucks, an expansion team formed in 1968, received national attention for drafting Lew Alcindor, UCLA's three-time NCAA champion and perhaps the greatest college player in history, with the first pick in the first round of the 1969 draft. Right out of the gate Alcindor dominated the league. He played like a god among mortals. Tall yet fluid, skinny yet strong, as a rookie he averaged almost thirty points a game. He helped the Bucks go from one of the worst teams in the NBA to a playoff contender, as the Bucks made it all the way to the 1970 Eastern Conference finals.

Alcindor's second year in the league, the Bucks acquired the Big O, Oscar Robertson, from the Cincinnati Royals. Drafted out of the University of Cincinnati in 1960, Robertson was one of the most well-rounded players ever to step on a basketball court. A three-time college player of the year, he averaged a triple double his first five years in the league. (A triple double means a player scores ten or more points, rebounds, and assists in a game.)

The Michael Jordan of his era (although Jordan never averaged a triple double for an entire season—nor has anyone else), Robertson endured the worst type of hate playing in the Jim Crow South. On the road he wasn't allowed to stay in the same hotels as his white teammates, and he received regular death threats. White players who couldn't tolerate being outplayed by a Negro hid black cats in his locker before games. Understandably, Robertson turned inward and played angry.

He also took the lead on a crucial antitrust lawsuit against the league. In 1970, as the president of the NBA Players' Association, Robertson challenged the merger between the NBA and the ABA and demanded an end to restrictions on free agency. The suit sought payment for players caused harm by the NBA's option clause. *Robertson v. National Basketball Association* was battled in court for six years and delayed the NBA-ABA merger until 1976. It won players the right to become free agents, which drove up all players' salaries. This lawsuit, more than anything I can think of, helped free players from the control of the owners. Robertson won nearly every award you could win as a basketball player—Rookie of the Year, MVP, scoring titles, and a championship ring—but spearheading and eventually winning this lawsuit was his greatest professional accomplishment. He also helped prove that unions were absolutely necessary in any line of work, including professional sports.

On the court the Bucks were unstoppable. The team beat Earl "the Pearl" Monroe, Wes Unseld, and the rest of the Baltimore Bullets four games to one in the 1971 NBA Finals, and Robertson finally had his championship. The autumn after the Bucks won the championship, Lew Alcindor publicly revealed that he had changed his name to Kareem Abdul-Jabbar his senior year at UCLA. Inspired by a devotion to Islam, his feelings of alienation from the white race, and Muhammad Ali's decision in 1964 to change his name from Cassius Clay, Kareem made the courageous, follow-your-heart decision.

I remember my uncles expressing their support for Kareem around the dinner table. "You know, Kareem's name change is about carving out a space for Black people as much as it is about religion. This is a political calculation, too," said my Uncle Bruce. Kareem couldn't be mentioned without Uncle Bruce invoking Muhammad Ali. It wasn't lost on my uncles that Ali's affiliation with the Nation of Islam helped give him the moral fortitude and confidence to become increasingly more political and outspoken on issues that affected the entire Black race. "No man, not even Ali, is an island," Uncle Bruce would say.

Kareem's name change elevated him to the heights of Ali as far as my uncles were concerned. Although Kareem was often depicted as being aloof and a loner by the press—Kareem and Oscar Robertson carried the burden of racism similarly—he would talk about the history and the plight of Black people in post-game press conferences.[6] Because he would speak his mind, reporters were scared of Kareem. My need to use my status as an athlete to speak out against the injustices targeting my people seemed to intensify after moving to Milwaukee, as if memories of my uncles discussing Kareem, Robertson, and Ali over the dinner table were flooding back to me.

My first year with the Bucks (the 1984–1985 season), my third year in the league, I started all eighty-two games at point guard. I joined Sidney Moncrief in the backcourt. Sid the Squid, as we called him, was a five-time All-Star and one of the preeminent shooters in the league, averaging more than twenty points a game during the height of his career. The Squid was also a relentless defender, winner of the league's first two Defensive Player of the Year awards. Playing with Moncrief, who had been featured dunking on the cover of *Sports Illustrated* in college, inspired my defense. We worked together as a well-trained unit.

Paul Pressey, Terry Cummings, and Alton Lister played up front. Lister and Cummings were the strategic keys to our offense. Lister had been the Bucks' first pick in the 1981 draft. As our seven-foot center, he averaged nearly ten points a game with eight rebounds. Terry Cummings earned his first All-Star appearance that year, averaging twenty-four points a game at power forward. We always tried to get the inside game going first. This would keep defenders off the shooters and leave the space for wide-open jumpers.

I fit in well with the Bucks. I averaged more than ten points a game, with a field goal percentage that hovered around 50 percent and roughly four assists a game. Working alongside Sid, I also had a career high of ninety-six steals that first season. I was a person the Bucks could count on—I was steady. What really made me feel at home was Coach Nelson's faith in my ability to shoot the three. He gave me the green light to let the ball fly. I went from shooting no more than 90 threes a season with the Clippers to more than 150 my first year and 225 my second year with the Bucks.

The number of threes taken in the NBA had risen steadily since the three-point line was introduced in the 1979–1980 season (the ABA had a three-point line as far back as 1967). There was a pushback against this rule change when it first was implemented, particularly among traditionalists. In the early '80s, teams were putting up only three or four three-pointers a game. Gradually, coaches began to warm to what the three could do for the game. By the mid-'90s clubs were shooting about fifteen a game. Now teams are shooting twenty-two a game, with guys like Steph Curry launching about eight a night.

It took some time for coaches to see that the squad that could make the most threes in a game more often than not would be the team that wins. Rick Pitino, coaching the New York Knicks in the late '80s, was the first to demonstrate to the rest of the league the power of the three. His Knicks squad averaged nearly 1,200 three-pointers a season while the rest of the league shot about 700. Pitino showed that not only could you win games, but you could also fill stadiums with the three. With the possible exception of a slam-dunk, few things fire up a crowd more than when an entire team heats up beyond the arc.

In my first year, the Bucks finished 36–5 on our home court and won our division during the regular season. We didn't dominate as the 1970–71 Bucks team had, but that '85 team was a force to be reckoned with. In fact—and here's a trivia answer for you—through the '80s, after the Lakers and the Celtics, the Bucks held the third-best winning percentage in the league. We certainly played better ball than the

Clippers, who finished eleventh in the Western Conference that year. We lost the Eastern Conference semifinals to the 76ers, after beating a rookie named Michael Jordan, as well as Dave Corzine, Orlando Woolridge, and the rest of the Chicago Bulls, in the first round.

CHAPTER 9

A DIFFERENT KIND OF BUSINESS

I heard a knock on my door on a lazy, cold February afternoon in 1987. I was recovering from a tiring ten-game road trip that had started in Chicago and wrapped up in San Antonio. After straining to lift myself from the couch, I opened the door and saw my brother-in-law Demetrius standing in the bitter winter air. He was with a young-looking brother who stood about my height and wore a Bulls hat balanced precariously on the back half of his head.

"Hey, Craig, this is my boy Robert, the guy I was telling you about. I think Carlita mentioned something to you?" Demetrius, one of Carlita's brothers, had been nagging me to listen to Robert sing for weeks. He'd met Robert at a Chicago El stop, where he was singing for change. Demetrius was always scheming, looking for that vein of gold that would take him the places he wanted to go. He was family, so I figured I'd give him and his latest prospect a few minutes.

They kicked the snow off their shoes and walked in to sit around our kitchen table. Carlita came downstairs, poured everyone lemonade, and greeted Robert warmly. Demetrius launched in. "As

I was telling you both, I was on my way to work a few months back and heard the rarest of voices filling the tube. I say to myself, who is this guy, and why is he down here in the dark singing for change? You two know how my mind works."

I looked up and saw Carlita roll her eyes. Demetrius continued, "Robert doesn't have two nickels to rub together. He's been sleeping on park benches and on couches. But the brother can sing."

Robert sat in shy silence, staring at his clasped hands. He was so young-looking that all the talk about his finances didn't feel rude. Rather, it seemed Demetrius was on a rescue mission, hoping to find a home for a lost orphan.

"Show Craig what you got," said Demetrius.

After a few more awkward moments of silence Robert stood up and belted out a song he had written himself. His voice was incredible.

"What did I tell you two?" said Demetrius. I was stunned. Robert had one of the best voices I have ever heard up close. It was rich and tuneful but also deeply pained. You could tell that Robert had been through the shit. Carlita seemed flushed, clearly impressed.

"Robert writes all his own material." Demetrius went on to describe how Robert's current manager was exploiting him and did very little work arranging gigs. It would cost $5,000 to free Robert from his contract, Demetrius said. It was clear that he hoped I would cut a check.

I didn't know the slightest thing about the music industry. Besides, the season was in full swing, and I didn't have the mental space to devote to this scenario. I looked at Robert and said, "Keep getting yourself out there. Inevitably you are going to stumble across someone who will see that your voice is worth much more than five thousand dollars." Robert nodded.

"We aren't looking for a manager, just a silent backer. Of course you'd get a cut of all of Robert's future earnings," Demetrius added.

"Yeah, I'm sorry, guys."

"We figured you'd need time to think about it," said Demetrius. Robert was back in silent mode.

Carlita invited them both to stay the night. After dinner, we smoked a little weed, watched a game, and were off to bed. The next morning they drove back to Chicago. Demetrius soon followed up by phone. There was no way I was going to shake this guy.

I told him to bring Robert's contract the next time they were in town. "I'll have my attorney look it over," I said. I was beginning to sympathize with Robert. He was from the Ida B. Wells housing projects and had been raised by just his aunts, in a family situation similar to my own.

The contract was a bad deal, according to my attorney. I figured if I went through with this, I'd want Carlita to be Robert's comanager. I couldn't help but see this as an opportunity to get her started in a career. She'd always wanted to be in the entertainment industry. Neither of us wanted a repeat of the isolation she'd felt in San Diego. Carlita was skeptical, but Robert's talent was undeniable. In spite of his shyness, you just knew he had a future. "Why not," she said, eventually. She'd learn about the music industry by jumping straight into the fire, along with Demetrius. More than anything, though, I think she empathized with Robert's situation. She had escaped the poverty of the ghetto, and, like me, she looked for any opportunity to get others out, particularly someone with Robert's talent.

We called Demetrius and told him the terms. He and Robert agreed; it wasn't as though they had a lot of other options. With that, I pulled out my checkbook and wrote a $5,000 check to liberate the nineteen-year-old singer who would one day become known to the world as R. Kelly.

* * *

My second year with the Bucks, Sidney Moncrief asked me if I wanted to take over his job as the team's players' representative. This job had a lot of turnover, as most guys failed to see the potential of the union. Drawing on the sage advice I'd received from Bill Walton in San Diego, I enthusiastically accepted. I saw being a players' rep as a platform for sharing the knowledge I had acquired at Long Beach. These meetings were not only opportunities for making sure we weren't being screwed by management but also brainstorming sessions for ways we could use our status as professional athletes to do some good in the community. The NBA players' representatives tended to be some of the most politically conscious men in the league. We met twice a year, once at All-Star weekend and then again in the postseason.

The eighties were a complicated time to be active in the area of racial justice. You had a guy like Jesse Jackson, a pillar of the civil rights movement—someone who stood mere feet away from Dr. King when he was shot—running for president of the United States. Jackson had a progressive campaign that acknowledged the plight and poor conditions of the majority of Black folks in the United States. In fact, Jesse was probably the first major presidential candidate to say, "Black lives matter." He made connections between the apartheid of South Africa and Palestine to the Jim Crow South. He discussed racism and economic inequality. However, he was trying to reroute the movement into the voting booth. I think after witnessing the wins and losses of the civil rights movement, the guy just threw up his hands and concluded the only way to make conditions better for Black folks is to work within the system and win small reforms.

I never saw the logic behind this attitude; it has always been so clear to me that our economic system is completely dependent on racism. The system needs a group of people who are seen as less than, a group of people who will bear the most intense burden when our economic system institutes a recession or a depression to restore

profits. To be sure, you can have a few Black people in power as long
as they are willing to preserve the status quo. It's never been hard
to find Black folks who are willing to sell out their race for a few
extra table scraps from the established white power structure—remember, there were plenty of Black slaves who managed the whip
on the plantations. A few Black people in high places also serve to
legitimize the system as a whole, and that is what we were contend-
ing with in the '80s.

The '80s were the early stages of so-called postracial America.
Our problems with race in this country had allegedly been cured,
as evidenced by the presence of Black politicians, like Chicago's
mayor, Harold Washington. Overt racism was substituted with code
words that masked business as usual. Now the language of "personal
responsibility" was used to keep inequality in place. According to
Ronald Reagan, "welfare queens" chose to live in poverty because
the government incentivized them to do so. Federal housing and
relief programs had to be dismantled so that people living in urban
ghettos could pull themselves up by their bootstraps, to freely enjoy
the benefits of "hard work."

The conditions of Black folks were viewed in a complete vacuum, if they were viewed at all. People stopped asking why Black
people were the first to be fired when jobs were sent overseas, or
the first people targeted in Reagan's War on Drugs, or the first dis-
placed by subprime loans and the destruction of public housing. It
was this tricky terrain that we tried to navigate over drinks at our
players' rep meetings.

$$* \quad * \quad *$$

Coach Don Nelson was the best thing that happened to me in Milwaukee. Nelly, as everyone called him, reminded me that winning was
what it was all about. He prepared us all season long for the playoffs,

expecting that we would make the postseason each year, and his teams usually rose to his challenge. After the final game of the regular season, Nelly would gather us all in the locker room and say, "Tell your wife, your girlfriend, whoever you're screwing, that you motherfuckers are mine now." He was joking but deadly serious at the same time.

Nelly won because he knew the importance of a strong defense. More than any of my previous coaches he taught me the value of defending the hoop. Working as a single unit on defense, a team of mediocre talent could transform into one that could slay giants. When you make defense a priority each trip down the court, you force an opposing offense to work harder to find open shots. Not only does a strong defense force bad shots and cause turnovers, but the opposing team also often lets their guard down, hoping to catch their breath, when it's their turn to play defense. This opens up the floor for easier shots for the team that is working harder on defense.

Strong defensive teams control the tempo of the game, so Nelly wanted us to be in physically better shape than any other squad. Because he placed such a strong emphasis on defense we were always running the fast break after we caused a turnover. This type of ball prepared me for Phil Jackson, Michael Jordan, and the Bulls, who were also a run-and-gun team that never forgot the importance of defense. I don't think I could have made the contributions I made to the Bulls if it hadn't been for Don Nelson.

* * *

When Robert wasn't in Chicago he was living in our spare bedroom in Milwaukee, which he quickly turned into a rat's nest. This annoyed Carlita, who claimed most of the housekeeping duties.

"Robert, if you're gonna stay here, you got to keep your damn room clean," she'd threaten. Robert would nod his head but wouldn't follow up. I wasn't much better, so I kept my mouth shut. I should have backed Carlita up. It was just one more thing that brought tension into the house. Robert was easy to be around, though. We spent a lot of time together, watching sports, talking basketball—he could hoop pretty well himself—and strategizing about his future.

"You'll see my name in lights one day. And I won't forget all that you two have done for me," he said often.

Carlita and Demetrius weren't having much luck booking Robert in large venues. The comanagers were working hard, though, and got him some small gigs, usually seedy clubs somewhere between Chicago and Milwaukee. The reality is, unless you're incredibly lucky, you need contacts in the music business, soft ones at least, to generate the necessary buzz to have your talent heard. I think experts would agree that very few people can cold-call their way to success in the music business. As the trio was beginning to feel desperate I picked up the phone, rang the Bucks' front office, and arranged for Robert to sing the national anthem at a game.

The day before Robert was scheduled to sing, Carlita took him to the mall and bought him a dark pinstriped suit. I think it was the first suit he ever owned. There was the possibility that someone in the crowd, or maybe someone watching at home on TV, would see Robert and give him his big break. On game day Carlita made all of us my regular pregame meal of beef tenderloin, baked potato, salad, and broccoli. Robert hardly touched his food and was quieter than usual.

After dinner the babysitter arrived to watch Jibril, and we drove to the MECCA Arena, home of the Bucks. Robert stayed quiet during the drive. "You nervous?" I asked, looking at him in the backseat through the rearview mirror.

"Nah, my stomach hurts a little, though."

"It's just nerves. You'll be fine." He nodded, and we listened to the radio the rest of the trip.

We arrived a few hours before tipoff for team warm-ups. Thirty minutes before game time I found Demetrius and Carlita, with two-year-old Jamaal, huddled around Robert near the Bucks' locker room.

"He's not singing, Craig," Carlita said, shaking her head and sighing.

"I'm not feeling good, man . . . my stomach still hurts…I don't want to throw up on the court . . . it doesn't look like I can do this tonight," Robert said, staring at the floor.

Carlita and Demetrius glared off into the distance.

I looked at Robert questioningly for a few seconds, took a deep breath, and said, "There will be other opportunities, my brother. Don't sweat it." Who was I to force Robert to do something he wasn't ready for? Sure, I had vouched for him. I was embarrassed to make the team scramble to find a replacement. But, at the end of the day, I was living my dream. Robert had a long way to go. Why make him feel smaller than he already felt?

I asked Carlita to drive Robert and Jamaal home. She was pissed but agreed. The Bucks used a recording of the anthem that night, and we handily beat the 76ers. I left the stadium feeling upbeat, blissfully ignorant of all that was going on between Carlita and Robert back at my house.

I'd later learn that this was the night that Carlita and Robert began a yearlong affair. They hid it well in the beginning. Eventually I started noticing abrupt silences between them when I walked unannounced into a room. Or I'd catch them smiling at each other in an all-too-knowing way. Part of me didn't want to acknowledge the infidelity because I couldn't bear the thought of putting my kids through a divorce. I had been faithful to Carlita to that point. I was wedded to the idea of Jamaal and Jibril growing up with a mom and a dad in the same house, and I didn't want to do anything to jeopardize that. Parenting is hard enough as it is. You need backup. In spite of all of her flaws, in spite of all my flaws, we generally worked well together.

I wanted to stay committed to Robert, but I found myself irritated by his presence around the house. I started to question whether or not he would ever get a break. One day he approached Carlita with a request for $9,000 to cover his expenses to be on the television talent show *Big Break*, hosted by Natalie Cole, whom I loved. I said no. I encouraged Carlita and Demetrius to keep putting in the legwork to promote Robert, and I said I'd continue to help him when I could, but I had to draw the line with the money. We were comfortable but by no means wealthy.

"If he wins, Robert promises that he would pay the money back. I'll even write up a contract," Carlita pleaded.

I was taken aback by her intensity. Carlita had initially been reluctant to loan money to Robert. She and Demetrius were clearly looking for a shortcut, but Carlita's sense of urgency seemed to come from a deeper place than simply business. Maybe I wasn't appreciating the impact *Big Break* could have on his career, I thought. How many contestants were there? What were the odds of winning? No one had clear answers. I was never much for gambling, and that's what this show seemed to be—a gamble. I continued to say no to loaning him more money, but Carlita went ahead and wrote Robert a check behind my back. She typed up the contract, as she said she would. Robert signed it—and won the contest.

We soon stopped seeing Robert around the house. Carlita felt betrayed by Robert, and she began to spend a lot of time alone in her room. A few years passed before I saw him at all. He never paid the money back. It didn't cross my mind to pursue him in court. I figured I was meant to be there for this person the world needed to hear at that moment in time. He was a Black urban success story and would soon rise to fame under his stage name, R. Kelly.

R. Kelly went on to do great and horrible things. Carlita and I were both proud to say we played a part in his musical success. The fact that he cheated with my wife, in my house, after all I did for him, still haunts me from time to time. My method of getting over painful things usually involves delving into the deeper motivations for people's actions, trying to understand them psychologically. I have also read enough religious texts to know that peace only comes through forgiveness. When stories about him and underage girls started coming out in the news, it affected me much worse than the cheating. I felt responsible in some way. With all that money he made, one would have hoped he would have found a good therapist to work through his issues.

We see each other now and again. We'll shoot hoops together, catch up, but we are not close in the way we used to be.

CHAPTER 10

BLINDSIDED

I signed a multi-year contract with the Bucks on November 1, 1987. I finally felt an ounce or two of security in the league, as the player with the highest three-point shooting percentage twice in three years: .451 in 1985–86 and .491 in 1987–88, a number that would have led the NBA even in these advanced three-pointer days of 2016.

Carlita still liked Milwaukee, and we began looking for a nicer home. In December of that same year, minister Louis Farrakhan called to let me know that he would be speaking at a Baptist church in Milwaukee later that winter. He and I both thought it would be a good idea to spread the word among my teammates. In the next couple months I talked periodically to the guys about my experiences with the Nation and why I thought they might benefit from hearing the minister speak. For those unfamiliar with the history of the Black struggle, I considered the Nation as good an entry point as any. There was general enthusiasm among the players and the feedback was positive.

On the day the minister spoke, a typically freezing-cold Saturday in mid-February, I was the only Buck in the church. I was

85

disappointed but not very surprised. What did come as a surprise was the fallout.

A week later, Carlita, Jamaal, Jibril, and I arrived home after a night at the circus. I clicked on the TV to watch the ten o'clock news. The first thing I heard was, "Coming up next, Bucks make a deal with Phoenix." Then it cut to commercial.

The phone rang. It was John Steinmiller, the Bucks' general manager, who, only a few months prior, had encouraged me to start house-hunting around Milwaukee.

"Hi, Craig. Sorry for the late-night call. How's the family?"

"What's up, John?" I asked, with a few butterflies in my stomach.

"Look, Craig. I'll get right to it. Management has decided to trade you to the Phoenix Suns. I wanted you to hear it from me before you hear it somewhere else."

He must have been watching the same news program, I thought. I didn't know what to say. I remained quiet.

"I'm sorry, Craig." Steinmiller gave no further explanation, other than it was in the best interest of both teams.

"Why did you tell me to start house-hunting if you knew I'd be traded?" I asked, trying to contain my anger.

"Again, I'm sorry, Craig. Maybe we can talk more tomorrow." He hung up.

The trade blindsided me. I was producing and getting good minutes with the Bucks. We were expecting another strong playoff run. Carlita was heartbroken.

Only a few days before I was scheduled to leave for Phoenix, Carlita and I took Jamaal, then three years old, to the doctor. Inexplicably, he had been walking with a limp and wetting the bed. X-rays revealed a tumor on the little guy's spine. We made an appointment with a cancer specialist, and I delayed my flight to Phoenix. After reviewing the X-rays the oncologist assured us the condition wasn't life-threatening, but any surgery on the spine, which Jamaal required, would be risky.

Despite the doctor's generally positive assurances, Carlita sobbed after we got home and put the kids to bed that night. A sinking feeling lingered in my stomach. We always worried about our kids, but this hit me at my core. I would be devastated if anything happened to either of our boys. I hated being so vulnerable. Carlita was disappointed at how reserved I seemed in the wake of the news, but acting stoic was my only response at the time. I tried to bury my fear, and Carlita resented me for it. Undoubtedly she was the stronger person for having the courage to express her feelings. I felt the distance between us grow even farther that day. We couldn't offer each other the support we both needed.

Jamaal came through the surgery fine but needed months of bed rest. He certainly couldn't make the move to Phoenix, at least not right away. Again, Carlita would be left alone, the weight of the world placed squarely on her shoulders. I offered to stay, but she insisted I go. She didn't want me taking any chances with my career, which was what was keeping the lights on and the medical bills paid. Some of our anxiety over Jamaal was alleviated when Carlita's sister Linda agreed to move into the house to help care for Jamaal. All I could think of was how this young kid would be confined to a bed when he should have been outside playing—while I would be 1,500 miles away.

I flew to Phoenix in a trade for six-foot-three shooting guard Jay Humphries. Upon my arrival I was placed on injured reserve. I was leading the NBA in three-point shots and perfectly healthy. *What the hell was the front office thinking?* I wondered. It made no sense.

Then I received a call from Tom Enlund, a sportswriter for the *Milwaukee Journal Sentinel*. "You know why you were traded," said Enlund.

"No, why?"

"The Bucks' front office didn't like all your dealings with Farrakhan."

"You've got to be kidding me. How'd you hear that?"

"A lot of guys are talking about it." He wouldn't name any names.

I was angry. I knew Farrakhan was generating all kinds of negative press. Ever since his trip to Libya to meet with Muammar Gad-
dafi in 1984, he'd had a target on his back with the mainstream media.
Farrakhan's mind-set was "An enemy of my enemy is my friend." He
also loved controversy, which that trip certainly generated. Farrakhan
had rightly been calling out Israel for occupying Palestinian lands.
The minister saw what was happening to those living in Gaza and
the West Bank as no different from what was happening in apartheid
South Africa to the indigenous African population, or what happened to Blacks in the Jim Crow South. Louis Farrakhan, for all his
faults, was demanding an end to Israeli apartheid long before many
others were.

The Nation of Islam was the sole resource at the time for those
who were looking for a revolutionary current in the Black struggle.
Where else were Black people gathering and organizing, the Con-
gressional Black Caucus? Their politics had long since been watered
down by corporate influence. With the Nation, I tried to take what
I needed and leave the rest. I saw the minister as a person who could
ignite discussion and debate—someone who could potentially tem-
per himself and communicate to a broader Black audience, or so
I hoped. Most importantly, he could organize and bring out the
numbers; the Million Man March proved that later on.

And a part of me hated the fact that another Black leader was
being so maligned in the press. Sure, the minister said things that
incensed people; there is no question the man was filled with passion and anger. Farrakhan regularly looked straight down the barrel
of the condition of the Black race in America, and the truth was
horrifying. Of course he was angry. There was so much hypocrisy

in the condemnation of Farrakhan, and few people seemed willing to talk about that. I thought that those who saw Farrakhan as the biggest problem the United States was facing needed to take a deep look at themselves, and their own hateful behavior, before they started casting stones at the minister.

At that point in my life, though, I wasn't going to the wall for Farrakhan, either. I was still developing spiritually and politically. I never called myself a Muslim, a Christian, a Buddhist, or anything for that matter. To this day I have never associated myself with any one religion. I wanted to walk in the shoes of as many people as I could. I did my best to learn about all the world's religions. At Long Beach State, I had studied the Torah so I could better understand what it was like to be Jewish, and I walked around campus in a yarmulke for a month. This experience had made me question Farrakhan's anti-Semitism. There had to be a better way. My goal was not just to talk the talk but to walk the walk. I was concerned about justice and freedom—not labels.

On the phone in Phoenix with Enlund, I tried to keep the mood light. "All I can say is that I wish the team the best in the playoffs. I hope they go all the way. If they win, I hope the team votes me some of their playoff winnings," I joked.

Enlund printed the part about playoff winnings but didn't mention the rumors about why I was fired. This was the first time my politics affected my career, which, in turn, affected my family and my future. It was disheartening. A young kid from the projects who scared the front office of an NBA team? The idea was difficult to comprehend. I felt the structure must be built on shaky foundations if someone like me could be perceived as threatening.

You always hear about how a player needs to be loyal to a team. Unfortunately, we rarely hear about a team's obligations to its players. There is a moralism at play with the athletes (in recent years, think of LeBron James's decision to leave Cleveland to play for the

Miami Heat), but no such standard applies to the owners. The Bucks' front office never sat down with me to discuss my politics or spiritual beliefs. No one ever asked me why I was associated with the Nation of Islam. My answer would have been sincere, forthright, carefully thought through, and nuanced—if anyone had bothered to ask. And I would have been open to better ideas if presented with any.

I gave my all for the Bucks each night. My family was settled in Milwaukee. We loved being so close to our extended family in Chicago. It was frightening to realize that I had so little control over the direction of my career. If Tom Enlund was correct—Sam Smith, in his book *The Jordan Rules*, would confirm Enlund's assertion—and I was traded for the reasons above, and I believe he was, then the message from the Bucks' front office was clear: follow your conscience and speak openly about it . . . and risk everything. On a positive note, the Bucks management proved I could make waves. I had a voice that could be heard. I felt empowered on another level.

My unexpected release from the team was made much clearer when I learned about a tragic event that had occurred a decade and half earlier. On January 18, 1973, Kareem Abdul-Jabbar's spiritual mentor, Abdul-Khaalis, and his wife and children were killed in their Washington, DC, townhouse—a building owned by Kareem—by Muslim extremists. The Bucks were forced to provide security for Kareem throughout the 1973 season—in addition to dealing with the FBI—because they thought the same extremists would target Kareem. Fear of Muslims stemming from this episode was still prevalent in Milwaukee, and my activities with the Nation of Islam undoubtedly dredged up bad memories within the Bucks organization.

The 1987–88 season was winding down, and the Suns had no hope of making the playoffs. I needed to get back into a regular playing routine to keep my mind off the helplessness I felt being so far away from my family. But I only sat on the bench. NBA Hall of Famer Jerry Colangelo, the Suns' general manager at the time, didn't have many answers for me. The Bucks clearly wanted me gone, and I think they turned to the Suns because they knew I was close with Jerry. "Mr. Colangelo," as I still thought of him, went to Bloom High School with my Aunt Edna, and we had stayed in touch as I came up in the league.

There were also rumblings that the Bulls were looking for a shooting guard to take some of the pressure off Michael Jordan. Because the Bucks and the Bulls were division rivals, a direct trade between the two teams would have been unlikely. This was only speculation, though; I was in the dark, trapped in the desert, forced to bide my time and see what happened after the season.

To my surprise, I was taken off the injured reserve list and played the final ten games of the season with the team. The day after the last game Jerry called me into his office and said, "Craig, I have an opportunity. I think it will be good for you. How would you like to go back to Chicago to play for the Bulls? What do you think?"

"Come on, Jerry, you know that's not a decision I need to think about!" I said.

The Bulls were my team as a kid. My first trip to Chicago Stadium was in 1972, when I was twelve years old. Mr. Roseborough, my seventh grade teacher at Gavin, took me and a few other kids from the class. Mr. Roseborough was a true mentor who knew there were lessons to be had not just in the classroom but out in the world. On a Saturday morning, we all squeezed into his red Volkswagen Beetle to drive down to the stadium. The Bulls were playing the New York Knicks—Walt Frazier, Willis Reed, a guy on the bench named Phil Jackson, and the rest. Mr. R. paid for the tickets, and our parents gave us a few dollars for popcorn and a Coke. It was glorious. We sat in the nosebleeds, but I remember every detail of the game. The players ran back and forth as we watched through the haze of cigarette smoke that wafted up to the rafters amid the cheers and jeers.

The Bulls weren't a strong force in the league in the late '60s to mid-'70s, but I kept close tabs on Norm Van Lier, Bob Love, Chet Walker, Bob Weiss, and Jerry Sloan. I was particularly inspired by "Stormin' Norman" Van Lier. At only six-one he was the most tenacious player on the court. He swarmed players—usually bigger than he was—on defense and was named to the NBA All-Defensive team three times. What made this feat all the more impressive is that it took place in the final years of his career. To play hard, night in and night out, in the early part of a career, trying to prove you are worthy of the league, is one thing. To play tough defense in the twilight of a career is what I admired. Van Lier always seemed to be learning on the court, figuring out how he could contribute. His ego never got in the way of his overall game. I also figured I wasn't going to be much taller than Norm. If I was going to make it I had to hustle just as hard.

My friends and I left the stadium itching to get on the court back at Gavin. We were ready to make names for ourselves. Every part of my being wanted to be on that stadium floor one day, and I trusted the little voice inside my head that promised it was possible.

I saw the Bulls play again the following year in September. They played an exhibition game against the Phoenix Suns at Bloom High. Future Hall of Famer Connie Hawkins, a six-foot-eight power forward for the Suns, was the first player to enter the gym. I was five-foot-nothing, less than a hundred pounds at the time, so to see Connie run up and down the court in warm-ups was an awesome and wondrous sight. I was halfway up the stands, but you could feel the wind generated by all these giants as they ran up and down the court and loudly squeaked their gym shoes as they cut across Bloom's freshly polished floor. Sitting so close, I could see the claw marks the players were inflicting on the basketball. (NBA players do more damage to basketballs than people know.) My proximity to the players was intimidating yet made everything concrete. Yes, these guys were huge, but they sweated, they laughed, they were human.

* * *

Tex Winter, my coach and mentor from Long Beach State, was the assistant coach for the Bulls at the time of the trade. Tex had befriended Jerry Krause, the Bulls' general manager, when Krause was an NBA scout and Tex was at Kansas State. In an interview Tex once said,

> One day, I was watching TV, and I saw that the Bulls were introducing their new general manager, Jerry Krause, who, some years before, as a young NBA scout, had come many times to Kansas State. And he used to tell me: "When I become an NBA executive, I will hire you, because I want to use your offensive system." I told my wife, Nancy: "Look at this man. He's going to call me within 24 hours." And he did! He called me the following morning, at about 7:30.

Tex made the trade feel like a true homecoming. Although most people, including me, thought it was Tex who initiated the deal, it was assistant coach Johnny Bach who lobbied Jerry Krause to sign me. Bach thought I would spread the defense, and Tex vouched for me. The Bulls had Michael Jordan, probably the greatest basketball player in the world, but he needed help. He was continually being double- and sometimes triple-teamed because no one could guard him one on one. Jordan, at this point in his career, was a slasher. He took the ball to the hoop better than anyone. It wasn't hard to visualize MJ driving the lane and kicking it out to me in the corner for the open three. I'd be the shooter the Bulls could depend on.

Doug Collins, the head coach, had gone to school with my Uncle Larry at Illinois State, so he knew my family. Couple that with the presence of Tex Winter, and it seemed the stars were aligned for the Bulls and me. The basketball experience I had waited for my entire life had arrived.

CHAPTER 11

COMING HOME

I had played in Chicago Stadium at 1800 West Madison before, but I was returning to that legendary court for the 1988–89 season as a six-year NBA veteran and a member of the Chicago Bulls. Built in 1929, the arena by today's standards was a dump, yet the flaws felt sacred somehow. The floor was creaky and unusually cold because of the hockey ice below the boards. The locker rooms were musty, like a sweaty basement. I savored every inch of the place.

They called it the Madhouse on Madison because our fans were wild-eyed, barking animals. They frothed at the mouth equally out of a love for us and a loathing for whomever we played. With its ancient acoustics, Chicago Stadium did not absorb sound well. The concrete, steel, and smoke-stained plaster walls only amplified the maniacal screams of the crowd. The stadium's Barton organ had a force equivalent to twenty-five hundred-piece brass bands. The stereo system was even louder.

I try to tell friends what it was like when the lights went dark and the spotlight circled to the slow-building electric sounds of "Sirius" by the Alan Parsons Project, and the eardrum-shattering roar of our fans as our starters emerged onto the hardwood, but I can never find the words. It was a transcendent experience for me, and the noise still echoes in my dreams. If we were tired after a long road trip our fans always managed to raise us up. I didn't fully grasp it at the time, but this was the golden age of basketball, and I was playing on what would become the most golden of teams.

Success didn't happen overnight for the Jordan-era Bulls. There were questions raised by the media about whether MJ could win it all and whether he could handle the pressure of the latter rounds of the playoffs. That was the problem. Of course he couldn't. Not even Michael Jordan, the Zeus of basketball, could win a championship alone. Jerry Krause had been trying to find the right ensemble for him for years. Before Scottie Pippen, the multi-position player from the University of Central Arkansas, and Horace Grant, the power forward from Clemson, arrived in 1987, Brad Sellers and Charles Oakley were Michael's main wingmen. It took time to get the cast right.

But even with Scottie and Horace the Bulls needed more depth. They wanted someone tall who could complement Jordan's defensive aptitude. Krause found the perfect fit in Bill Cartwright, the seven-foot-one center from San Francisco, who was picked up from the Knicks in a trade for Charles Oakley the same year as me. Bill was the third overall pick in the 1979 draft, and he'd averaged seventeen points and almost eight rebounds a game with the Knicks two years before he was traded to the Bulls. Oakley and Jordan were close friends, and Jordan fought the trade. They found out about it on a trip to Las Vegas to see a Mike Tyson fight. Jordan wasn't happy. Cartwright's value would soon become apparent, though. With the wingspan of a military transport plane, Bill would provide suffocating defense and a strong offensive presence down low in the paint. Cartwright never averaged as many rebounds as Oakley, but he filled a crucial role, and was more well-rounded.

Horace Grant was also developing fast enough to make up for Oakley's dominance on the boards. But the Bulls needed even more to make it to the top of the mountain. A championship team demands a deep bench that can play cohesively with the starters. Along with John Paxson, who had been with the team since 1985, Stacey King, Will Perdue, B. J. Armstrong, Scott Williams, and Cliff Levingston would eventually complete the puzzle and pave the way for a dynasty.

I knew right away that we were going places. You had to be part of a Bulls practice to understand. Michael Jordan's leadership and drive—not just to be the best player in the world but to be on the best team in the world—made every practice as intense as, if not more intense than, our games. It's one thing to play on a team with a competitive coach who says all the right things to fire everyone up, like Don Nelson did in Milwaukee. But the team enters a different headspace when it has a player who has all the otherworldly talents and leadership skills of Jordan but also the competitive drive of . . . well, Michael Jordan. There is no analogy for Jordan's competitiveness. The drive he possessed is a thing unto itself.

Jordan would finish his career as a fourteen-time All-Star, ten-time NBA scoring champ, five-time MVP, six-time NBA champ, and six-time finals MVP. He was the hardest-working athlete I have ever seen. His determination rubbed off on nearly everyone. For Jordan each practice was an opportunity to anticipate a game-time scenario. With each tipoff in front of an actual crowd we felt relaxed and prepared because we had seen the situation over and over again in practice. Because Jordan practiced as passionately as he played in games, we replicated not just the plays but the emotional intensity as well.

From free-throw competitions in practice, golf, and card games to making the game-winning shot in the final seconds of a playoff game, Jordan embraced each challenge with nearly the same energy. Jordan had a way of elevating each player to his own level of intensity. When he told someone to execute a play a certain way, players did it because they had seen him do it harder and better.

He drove some of his teammates nuts. If you were wrong he let you know it. Jordan wasn't afraid to tear into someone when he thought they were messing up a play or thought they were loafing. Sometimes Jordan would hound a guy all week long. I have never seen one man hound another man as acutely as Jordan did Brad Sellers. Sellers, a seven-foot, wiry power forward, had led the Big Ten in rebounds at Ohio State, but he had a hard time with the stronger guys in the NBA. Jordan felt that Brad, the Bulls' first-round draft pick in 1986, wasn't playing up to his potential and pounced on him like a lion pounces on a wounded giraffe. Jordan's goal in life, it seemed, was to dominate everyone else who stepped on the court. If he noticed the slightest weakness in a person's personality he would mercilessly exploit it. Brad couldn't deal with MJ's intensity and was eventually run off the team after the 1988–89 season. He was a great guy with a deep intellect, who eventually ended up mayor of Warrensville Heights, Ohio.

Most guys were hungry for Jordan's approval, even the players on other teams, which made opposing coaches like New York's Jeff Van Gundy livid. Of course it wasn't like that with everyone. One time Jordan called out Bill Cartwright in a practice with particular ferocity. Bill pulled Michael off to the side and said, "If you ever talk like that to me again, I will break both your knees and you'll never play another game."

Jordan didn't intimidate me either. He respected me because I never bowed down to him. After a loss in Orlando one night, Jordan, who'd scored fifty points or so, entered the locker room kicking chairs, cursing, and slamming doors. "We should have won that fucking game!" he kept saying.

After his tantrum, there were a few seconds of silence. I broke it. "You finished? Because you aren't the only one who is pissed, brother. Did you stop to consider that maybe we would have won if you passed the ball more? Horace, Scottie, Bill, and myself were open all night. Maybe the score would have been different if you looked up a few more times, bruh."

The locker room went silent and Jordan responded, somewhat passively, "We still should have won."

In a lot of ways, I relied on my education to maintain my edge with Jordan. I knew he didn't know shit about Black history. No matter how much people praised Jordan, no matter how many awards he won, no matter how much money he had, he didn't have the thing I held most dear: an education in the struggle of our people. This gave me confidence on the court and in the locker room with him.

I needed that confidence. Our practices were so intense we'd sometimes run for just forty minutes before we had to call it a day. It was a competitive environment at the Deerfield Multiplex, where we practiced, but we always tried to keep things light when walking out of the gym each day. Scottie Pippen and Horace Grant, who were joined at the hip, were good at helping the team decompress after a practice. They'd regularly ask Jordan if they could borrow his comb—things like that. All anyone wanted to do was win championships and we didn't need any tension getting in the way.

It would take two losses to the Pistons in the Eastern Conference finals in consecutive years—and a new head coach in Phil Jackson—for us to realize our full potential as a unified team, though. It also took Jordan's learning the importance of listening to all the voices on the team. When you feel heard by someone you feel more like an equal. When he finally realized this, he helped us relate to his strengths and overcome our own weaknesses.

My first season with the Bulls was decent, but by no means were we championship caliber yet. We went 47–35 in the regular season. My first night wearing #14 in the Bulls' red, white, and black, I touched the ball three times and went three for three from behind the three-point line. John Paxson, a two-time All-American and academic All-American from the University of Notre Dame, who would average seven points and 3.6 steals a game throughout his nine seasons in the league, had the assists. I played forty-nine games and averaged about twenty-two minutes and ten points a game that season. I would have played more, but my regular season was cut short by an ankle injury. We made it to the playoffs, for which I was back but still not a hundred percent.

The sportswriters were saying we didn't have a chance against Cleveland, our opponent in the first round. Jordan pulled a Joe Namath and guaranteed we would win the series in four games. Coached by Hall of Famer Lenny Wilkens, the Cavaliers were a confident team with a deep bench. Mark Price, Larry Nance, Brad Daugherty, John "Hot Rod" Williams, Ron Harper, and Craig Ehlo were the soul of the squad. Led by Price, who was an extension of Wilkens on the court, the Cavs went from a 42–40 record in the 1987–88 season to a 57–25 record in 1988–89.

Price was soft-spoken but usually managed to daunt his opponents. In spite of being only six feet tall, he never backed down or gave up. Not even Jordan scared him. Price had incredible court vision. A lot of people think being a top-notch point guard is all about having good instincts and being quick. The best point guards study the game; they know the offense inside and out. Then they master the ball handling and passing techniques that allow them to execute. First-rate point guards aren't born; they are made.

The Bulls had beaten the Cavs in the first round of the playoffs the previous year. Entering the series in '89 we were poised, but we had seen enough tape and played the Cavs enough times to know how well they had gelled as a team over the course of a year. As the sportswriters predicted, it was a grueling, bang-up series for us. The

Cavs spoiled Jordan's bold four-game prediction by taking us to the fifth game, but Jordan would have the final word.

The fifth game of the series was tight throughout. I played much of the game and was two for four from behind the three-point line. It is the final minutes of the game, however, that will be seared into my mind the rest of my life. Michael Jordan put us ahead with a clutch jumper from just above the block with six seconds to go. We were up 100 to 99. We thought we had it in the bag. Our bench was jumping up and down and Richfield Coliseum was blanketed in silence.

With only six seconds on the clock, for the next play I was tasked to guard Craig Ehlo, who was taking the ball out of bounds at center court. The crowd boomed back to life. The referee blew the whistle. As I jumped up and down Ehlo threw the ball past my right ear to Larry Nance at the top left elbow. Ehlo ran behind my back on the give-and-go and took a handoff back from Nance for the easy layup. I dropped my head, grabbed the ends of my shorts, and started swearing to myself under the basket. I had broken the cardinal rule: never take your eyes off the person inbounding the ball. I could hear Doug Collins screaming at me. My mistake lost the game. I wasn't about to let myself blame my sore ankle. There were only three seconds left on the clock.

As I walked back to the bench, still cussing at myself, MJ grabbed the back of my jersey and said in a hoarse yet sure voice, "I got you Hodge. It's all right. We got this." We left the huddle with a play that had Brad Sellers inbounding the ball for us at midcourt. I ran to the corner and waited for a possible kick-out jumper. We knew Jordan would be double-, maybe triple-teamed. Sellers passed the ball to Jordan a few feet above the three-point line in heavy traffic. Jordan drove and pulled up for a jump shot just above the foul line over Ehlo. . . . *It's good!* The crowd was stunned back to silence. Jordan nearly jumped into the rafters with his famous fist pump. We won the series!

The Bulls ran back to the locker room. Jordan quieted everyone down and said, "Hodge, tell 'em what I told you." I told them. Jordan's buzzer beater would forever be known as "The Shot." It's the shot that Gatorade chose for their "Be Like Mike" advertising campaign. It was that shot that would seal the series against a tough Cavalier team and help us roll into New York against the Knicks. It was the shot that saved me from becoming the Bill Buckner of the Bulls.

We played some of our best basketball of the year against an aggressive Knicks team in the Eastern Conference semifinals. Rick Pitino coached Patrick Ewing, Mark Jackson, Gerald Wilkins, Johnny Newman, and Charles Oakley to a strong 52–30 regular season record. The Knicks had won their first division championship since Phil Jackson played on the team in 1970. The team was hungry. Oakley was there to help Ewing grab the offensive rebounds and kick the ball out to Jackson and Newman for the three.

The Chicago fans hated this Knicks team. Mark Jackson, the 1988 Rookie of the Year, and Ewing irritated them the most. Jordan had a particular loathing for Mark Jackson's flamboyant, cocky play. Collectively, however, the Bulls had nothing but respect for the Knicks. Both teams felt they had something to prove. The series was hard-fought, but we won four games to two. Assistant coaches John Bach and Jim Cleamons had drilled it into us that defense would be the key to victory, and we heeded their advice. We swarmed the boards and didn't give up any easy shots. We were on to Detroit to face the "Bad Boy" Pistons in the Eastern Conference finals, and we were riding high.

✱   ✱   ✱

NBA players find flashy brochures selling luxury real estate, high-end cars, jewelry, electronics, and more littering the locker rooms of the league. One of these ads had caught my eye. "FORTY ACRES!" it read in bold across the top of the brochure. The size of the lot seemed to be speaking to me directly. *I wonder if a mule comes with the property?* I thought to myself. I began reading: swimming pool, full-court indoor basketball court, modern farmhouse, all for just $190,000. I sat there, envisioning my boys running around barefoot on the property.

I went home and made an appointment for Carlita and me to drive out and see the farm. Carlita fell in love with the place on the spot. The drive from Walkerton, Indiana, to Chicago Heights was only an hour and a half. Our families could visit. We purchased the farm after only two showings. The boys took to it right away. We spent weekends and summers relaxing, reading, working out, and enjoying each other's company. The farm was the best thing I bought with my NBA money. I wish it were still mine.

Me during my junior year at Rich East High School, in 1977
(*Chicago Heights Star*)

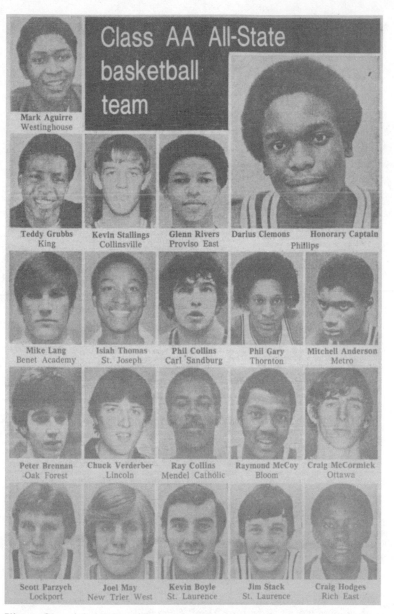

Class AA All-State basketball team

Mark Aguirre
Westinghouse

Teddy Grubbs
King

Kevin Stallings
Collinsville

Glenn Rivers
Proviso East

Darius Clemons

Honorary Captain
Phillips

Mike Lang
Benet Academy

Isiah Thomas
St. Joseph

Phil Collins
Carl Sandburg

Phil Gary
Thornton

Mitchell Anderson
Metro

Peter Brennan
Oak Forest

Chuck Verderber
Lincoln

Ray Collins
Mendel Catholic

Raymond McCoy
Bloom

Craig McCormick
Ottawa

Scott Parzych
Lockport

Joel May
New Trier West

Kevin Boyle
St. Laurence

Jim Stack
St. Laurence

Craig Hodges
Rich East

Illinois Class AA All-State Team for 1978, with me at bottom right (*Chicago Sun-Times*)

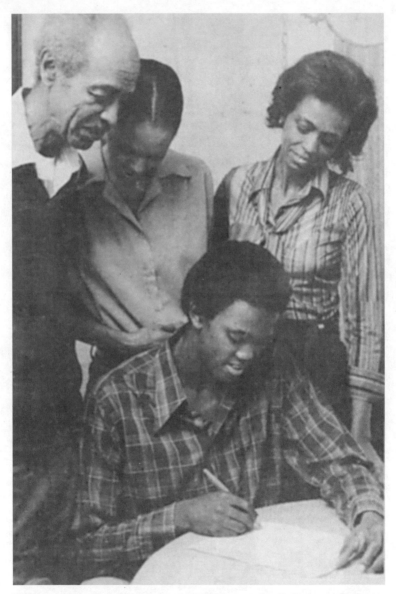

Signing to go to Long Beach State, in 1978, as my family looks on. Left to right: Granddad; my sister, Lori; Mom (*Chicago Heights Star*)

Left to right: Jamaal, Jibril, and Carlita (photo by Magic Photo at River Oaks Mall, 1999)

Larry Bird and I in the final round at my first three-point contest, in Dallas in 1986 (photo by Robert Furnace)

Isiah Thomas guarding me in Detroit in 1991 (photo by Robert Furnace)

My dad, my sister, and I after I won my second of three consecutive three-point contests, in Charlotte, NC, in 1991 (photo by Robert Furnace)

Operation UNITE meeting in December 1991

Cliff Levingston and I at All-Star weekend, 1991, in Orlando
(photo by Robert Furnace)

Coaching at Chicago State in 1995 (photo by Robert Furnace)

Me as a junior at Long Beach State during the 1980–1981 season (courtesy of Long Beach State)

Tex Winter coaching at Long Beach State (courtesy of Long Beach State)

Shooting hoops at the White House in a dashiki in 1992 after the Bulls won our second national championship (courtesy of the George Bush Presidential Libary)

CHAPTER 12

THE PISTONS

Hailing from the neighborhood of Lawndale on Chicago's West Side, Isiah "Zeke" Thomas had been Chicago's most beloved hometown basketball hero for as long as I can remember. I didn't play against him until I was on the Clippers, but my good friend Raymond McCoy, a McDonald's All-American, had run up against Isiah regularly in national tournaments and All-Star games. Raymond gave me the inside scoop on Isiah's game throughout high school, and the intel always stirred a little jealousy and a lot of admiration. Isiah woke up at 4 a.m. and commuted ninety minutes each way to St. Joseph High School in Westchester, Illinois, to play for the fabled coach Gene Pingatore, the winningest head coach in Illinois high school basketball history. In only his junior year, Isiah led St. Joe's to the state finals. The following year Isiah was selected for the Pan American Games team and the 1980 Olympic team.[7]

In contrast to his saintly smile, Isiah was the toughest, meanest, and best high school basketball player in Chicago, possibly in the country. Only six-foot-one, Thomas stood toe to toe with anyone. He invoked fear in his opponents because of his street smarts, aggressive play, leadership skills, and talent. His ability to overcome his height limitations, his tumultuous family life (two of his brothers died tragically), and economic background instilled hope in countless young players throughout Chicago and beyond.

Isiah's stature in the Windy City was elevated further after his Indiana University team won the NCAA championship his sophomore year with Isiah as a consensus All-American. When Zeke was drafted as the second overall pick in 1981 by the Detroit Pistons, Chicagoans felt immense pride that Zeke was one of their own. Even after Jordan arrived in 1984, Chicago basketball fans still rooted for Isiah. In early June 1987, however, Isiah's preeminence in the city vanished seemingly overnight, replaced by Jordan.

In the Eastern Conference finals in 1987, the Pistons lost to the Celtics in a hard-fought, tension-filled seven-game series. In a locker room interview after the series, Dennis Rodman said, in his now famous, loose-tongued way, that Larry Bird "was very overrated," and had won three league MVPs "because he [was] white." Asked his opinion of Rodman's statement, Isiah, rather than distancing himself from the comment, agreed with Rodman. "Larry Bird is a very good player, but if he was Black he would be just another good guy," Thomas said. Rodman was a rookie and a headstrong eccentric, so no one cared too much about what he had to say, but Isiah was the league's golden boy, with a million-dollar smile, limitless talent, insane work ethic, and legendary charisma. Nobody expected him to step out of line.

Many soon forgot that Rodman had initiated the controversy. Isiah, as the leader of the team, backed up his teammate and probably believed the comments to be true, but I doubt he imagined the breadth and scope of the press coverage and the vicious backlash that would follow. During the finals Isiah was forced to participate in a joint press conference with Larry Bird in the hopes of putting the issue to rest. He said he was "joking" but didn't back down much. Isiah wanted the press to acknowledge that racial stereotypes existed. He, rightly, was annoyed by the emphasis placed on Larry Bird's "work ethic" and that of many prominent white players. Isiah, along with others such as myself, was frustrated by how often Black players are characterized as "naturally gifted" or "possessing God-given talent"—as if Black athletes don't work their asses off to play at the highest levels. To me Isiah's debacle with the press was additional proof that one can never underestimate the enduring legacy of racism in America. It was also a message to Black players: don't ever mention race in the NBA. Isiah never recovered his golden-boy image, despite his continued dominance on the court.

The Pistons, however, gelled under the intense scrutiny and media attention. In the 1988–89 season they posted the best record in the NBA, with sixty-three wins and nineteen losses. Bill Laimbeer, Rick Mahorn, John Salley, Mark Aguirre, Dennis Rodman, Joe Dumars, and Isiah had always played tough and aggressive; the team as whole, though, turned genuinely bad, exaggerating the down-and-dirty image the media had hyped in the wake of Rodman's and Isiah's comments. The players took to wearing Oakland Raiders–inspired gear in most interviews (the Raiders were the bad boys of the NFL) and they began dishing out harder fouls and initiating even more fights during games. Detroit became an "us-against-the-world" team, yet there was a method to their madness.

We lost all six games against the Pistons during the regular season—although the last few were close, with the final game coming down to two points in overtime. But our impressive showing against Cleveland propelled us into the match-up against Detroit in the Eastern Conference finals. The Pistons, having destroyed the aging Celtics and a strong Milwaukee Bucks team in the previous series, implemented the infamous "Jordan Rules" against us.

The Jordan Rules were an attempt to disrupt Michael Jordan's game by double-teaming him, forcing him to his left off the dribble, and hitting him hard every time he drove to the hoop. In spite of the Pistons' tongue-in-cheek denial that they existed, the Jordan Rules were a very real set of tools Detroit used to uproot our team's chemistry. If a Bull took a hard foul by Laimbeer, Rodman, Mahorn, or Thomas, we took it personally, and this was exactly what the Pistons wanted. Detroit could crawl inside a player's head better than any other team. Once they were worming around, we stopped functioning as a single unit, and the game turned into an individual pissing match.

We came out strong, defeating Detroit for the first time all year in game one, 94–88. We lost game two, won game three by two, and lost game four, despite a forty-six-point effort from Michael. I had my best game in game five, shooting five for five from behind the three-point arc. Jordan only had eighteen that game. The press asked if Doug Collins was using MJ as a "decoy" that game. Far from it; Jordan was burned out. Collins relied on "The Black Cat," the team's nickname for Jordan (I called him The General) probably a bit too much. Collins ran one isolation set after another, letting Jordan do his thing, but Michael was exhausted. In a way, that was what Jordan wanted. At that point in his career, he felt like he had to do it all. I think this played right into the Pistons' hands, in their attempt to unravel us as a team.

There had been a period that season when things were different. I was starting at shooting guard, and Michael was at the point guard position. It was much harder to double- and triple-team him when he was in the middle of the court, so he didn't have to work as hard on offense. During this stretch I doubled my career average, pointwise, to produce eighteen points a game. With this strategy, we won ten out of eleven games on a West Coast road trip. Jordan was phenomenal. He had seven triple doubles in a row. I went twenty-two for thirty-three from behind the three-point line.

Don Nelson, my coach with the Bucks, who was now coaching Golden State, came up to me after a loss to us on the road trip and said, "Well, they finally figured it out there. I would have been playing [Jordan] at point guard from the day he showed up as a rookie."[8] The problem, however, was that Jordan didn't trust his team at that point, and I think he liked being the league's leading scorer. He didn't want to risk that. When I went down with an ankle injury, John Paxson stepped in and happily went along with Jordan's preference to play the two-guard position. And in the Eastern Conference finals, Detroit beat us by nine in a tough sixth game.

To their credit, the Pistons were physically and mentally stronger than we were, and their bench, led by Vinnie "The Microwave" Johnson, was too deep. Detroit went on to handily sweep the Lakers. We gave Detroit their only two losses in the 1989 playoffs, but no one could dispute that the Bad Boys were the most dominant team in the NBA that year.

$$* \quad * \quad *$$

Chicago fans were shocked by Bulls owner Jerry Reinsdorf's decision to fire head coach Doug Collins after the season. I was at home watching a Cubs game when I heard the news. I wasn't quite as surprised as the fans. Doug had an instinct for calling the right play at the right time, and there is no question that he helped transform the Bulls into a playoff contender. Collins was anxious, though, always intimidated by those he perceived as threats. He stopped talking to Phil Jackson for days on end, and even kicked Tex Winter out of practice for questioning one of his decisions. Many players felt that Doug reacted rather than planned. At thirty-seven, he was the youngest coach in the league, and he yelled to compensate for his inexperience and insecurity.

I loved Doug, though. I played some of the best basketball of my career when led by his excellent basketball instincts, like when he put me in the two-guard spot. He truly was one of the brightest

minds in the game. Unfortunately his basketball IQ didn't balance
out his volatility. Some said he wanted to be like Mike Ditka, who
led the Bears to a Super Bowl win in 1985—but he was unconvinc-
ing in the tough-guy role.

Reinsdorf and general manager Jerry Krause—who'd gone out
on a limb to bring Collins to the Bulls—and nearly every player
on the team knew the Bulls weren't going to find the cohesion and
pulse we needed to win championships under Doug. Players were
so incensed by him that they looked for ways to have him caught
in compromising positions—he was a big partier. Doug also had a
weapon in his arsenal that he wasn't using to his best advantage: Tex
Winter and his triangle offense.

Few tears were shed when Phil Jackson replaced Collins as
head coach that summer. Phil was his own man. He sure as hell
wasn't trying to be Mike Ditka. The culture of the team transformed
quickly under Phil, who stressed a concept, then little known, called
"mindfulness." Phil recognized that if a player understood exactly
who he was he could also understand his teammates better, which
would in turn give us perspective on the needs of the team as a
whole. If we understood our personal strengths and weaknesses
then we could intuit how to contribute to the team in a given moment, which sometimes meant sitting on the bench and encouraging those on the court. We learned to trust ourselves under Phil
because he trusted us. Phil loved to quote Rudyard Kipling's poem
The Law of the Jungle. I still recite this line to myself:

> For the strength of the Pack is the Wolf
> And the strength of the Wolf is the Pack.

Phil and I bonded right away. He gave me a book called *Way
of the Peaceful Warrior* by Dan Millman. It's a new-agey book about
staying present and following your bliss. Phil wasn't afraid of looking soft or strange, and I respected him for that. I remember a quote

from Millman's book that sums up Phil's philosophy of dealing with players: "Everyone tells you what's good for you. They don't want you to find your own answers. They want you to believe theirs." Phil had his ideas, but he wouldn't push them on you. If he wanted to say something deep to a player, he'd give him a book, usually before a long road trip. He gave Michael Jordan Toni Morrison's *Song of Solomon*, which opens with a character, an insurance agent, trying to fly off a roof but instead plummeting to his death. Yet the book ends with the line—so perfect for Jordan—"If you surrender to the wind, you can ride it."

Tex and Phil were close. Their connection cemented the philosophy that helped turn the Bulls into a dynasty. Tex's triangle aligned perfectly with Phil's spiritual approach to the game. We had three players who were always double- and sometimes triple-teamed: Michael Jordan, Scottie Pippen, and—although people don't remember this—Bill Cartwright. The triangle accounted for this. When a team ganged up on any of these players, B. J. Armstrong, John Paxson, and I were ready. We made it our goal to be 80 percent on open jump-shot opportunities when Michael or Scottie drove the lane—missing more than four shots out of twenty was unacceptable. And that's the way we talked about it. Our teammates made sure we never dropped below that number. Lighthearted but with an earnest undertone, Scottie came up to me after a miss on a few occasions to say, "Now I gotta be the shooter, Hodge?" I saw that as a challenge and made it my mission to have the best shooting percentage on the team.

NBA teams today have abandoned the triangle for the most part. Now there is a lot of perimeter play, with regular screen-and-rolls, with a big man at the top who is trying to turn the corner for an easy drive or kick out for a three-pointer. Teams are increasingly dependent on those who can dominate the game off the dribble, like LeBron, or someone who can the nail threes every time, like the Splash Brothers, Steph Curry and Klay Thompson. If the ball is on the wing rarely do you see anyone cutting from the backside of the defense the way Paxson, Scottie, MJ, and I used to do if Horace Grant or Bill Cartwright got the ball up top.

These days I most enjoy watching teams like the Spurs, who play basketball like a chess match. The Spurs use a derivative of the triangle called the dribble weave. A player dribbles down the sideline and hands off to a player on the wing or the hash mark; the player with the ball then dribbles back to the middle of the court, either to turn the corner at the top or, if he can't do that, to pass to the guy on the opposite wing, who can then spot up for a jumper or pass down low to Tim Duncan on the block. The Spurs understand midrange basketball, and they understand the importance of every player on a team committing to a system. It's one of the reasons they are a dynasty.

In the 1989–1990 season all we could think about was meeting Detroit again in the playoffs. During the regular season we fared better than the year before, with a 55–27 record. We beat Detroit in our first matchup, but they took every other game. The Pistons lost Rick Mahorn to the Minnesota Timberwolves in the expansion draft. Dennis Rodman entered the starting lineup partway through that season and thrived. Rodman hustled harder than any player in the league. There wasn't a loose ball he didn't dive after, a rebound he gave up on, or a charge he didn't take. Rodman, like so many other players in the league, was happy to escape the poverty of his upbringing. At this point in his career, he radiated a sense of gratitude and joy in every game. Propelled by Rodman's fire and intensity and Isiah's leadership, the Pistons finished the season 59–23.

The Eastern Conference finals were upon us before we could blink. It was another tough series. The Pistons continued to emphasize defense and discipline. We lost the first two games in Detroit, and Jordan took a hard fall in game two. But, somehow, he came back with eighty-nine total points in the next two games in Chicago. The series was now tied, two games to two. The Pistons beat us in Detroit, and we won again back in Chicago. Home court advantage proved to be crucial this series. We were reminded of the importance of the eighty-two regular season games: the best regular season record gets the home court throughout the playoffs, and Detroit made the most of theirs. The Pistons controlled the tempo in game seven. Physically, they were stronger than we were. I don't think we fully appreciated at that point how resilient a team needs to be to play all the way through the finals. Scottie Pippen came down with a debilitating migraine in game seven—we were all exhausted. In the final game of that series, we were blown out, 93 to 74.

We cried like babies in the locker room. No one, however, was ready to give up. The next season we were going to be adding some muscle mass. The Bulls' head trainer, Al Vermeil—brother of NFL coach Dick Vermeil—organized an early-morning workout regimen with Scottie, Michael, and B. J. Armstrong at Jordan's mansion in Highland Park. They called it the Breakfast Club—they'd hit the weights and then have breakfast. Bulking up helped improve their ability to overcome the hard hits Detroit laid on them each time they drove the paint or battled for a rebound.

I was one of the few players who stayed away from the weights that summer. I did a lot of pushups and crunches, but mainly I focused on stretching, a strength-building exercise in itself. I credited my commitment to flexibility as the key to my career's longevity. Mostly I didn't want anything messing with my shot.

The summer of 1990, I also had other issues on my mind. Jesse Jackson's organization, Operation PUSH, had organized a boycott of Nike. Nike did huge business in the Black community yet had no Black vice presidents, few Black employees, and almost no connections to Black-owned companies. I had been encouraging Jordan to break from Nike and go into the sneaker business for himself, with the aim of creating jobs in the Black communities whose residents were buying his product—Air Jordans, of course—in large numbers.

I'd brought this up with Michael on more than one occasion. "We need to start thinking about more meaningful ways to empower and raise our community up. Nike is paying some poor child in Vietnam or China slave wages to make your shoes. Does that sit well with you? Why shouldn't Black families reap the financial windfall that you are handing over to Nike? Nike would be nothing if it wasn't for you, General."

"I hear you, Hodge, I'm just not in a position to do that," Jordan would dismissively reply.

The Nike boycott embarrassed Michael and made his agent, the powerful David Falk, furious. Falk—whose nickname was "The Bird of Prey"—and Michael approached me that summer and asked me if I wanted to be president of the players' union. Such a high-profile position, with Michael's support, would provide me with greater job security. (It would be hard to oust the president of the union without a lot of undesirable attention.) Falk was one of the most powerful agents in the league. He had the ear of the owners and the other agents. Because I stood up for Black people and fought injustice, he and Michael knew I commanded respect around the league. I was a nice guy, too. I didn't have any enemies among the players.

However, I suspected that Falk hoped I'd be his rubber stamp. If the leaders in the union were silent about boycotts and other issues, he would be even more powerful. Beyond the boycott there were major negotiations around our pension plan. As a union rep for the Bulls, I was one of the most vocal proponents of an amendment to our contracts that would activate our pension benefits immediately after we retired, instead of being deferred until we were forty-five. Why should the owners reap the ten or fifteen years of accrued interest on our money? And many of the players needed that money.

Most knew nothing but basketball, and transitioning to the real world from the NBA, finding a job, and overcoming the injuries that many players were left with were serious challenges.

Pre-vote discussions showed near-unanimous support for the amendment. If it passed, however, teams would have to reduce their salary caps by $1.5 million. This, of course, would hurt Falk and the other agents' bottom line. Falk and his fellow reps received a 4 percent commission on contracts and stood to benefit substantially from increasing the salary cap, not reducing it.

I said no to Falk and Jordan. The amendment was passed overwhelmingly by the players' union. Walking out of the vote, I said to myself, *Falk and Jordan are going to run me out of the league.*

CHAPTER 13

THREE-POINT CHAMP

At the first three-point-shooting contest, in Dallas in 1986, Larry Bird burst into the locker room two minutes before the start of the competition, surveyed the scene, paused for an ominous moment, and then said matter-of-factly to me, Dale Ellis, Sleepy Floyd, Leon Wood, and the rest, "Who's comin' in second?" Larry then turned to Wood—a first-round draft pick for the 76ers in 1984 and a deadly shooter—and said, "Leon, I don't have to worry about you, you'll shoot yourself out of the competition in warm-ups." Larry's brash confidence could rattle mountains, but I let his words roll off my back. I knew I could outshoot anyone if I had the proper mind-set.

I surprised many in the opening round of the competition, scoring twenty-five points out of a possible thirty, a record that stood for nearly thirty years until Steph Curry broke it in 2014.[9] Each round lasted sixty seconds, and each player could launch twenty-five shots. There was a rack with five balls; the first four were worth one point, and the fifth, the "money ball," was worth two points.

Making that many shots was a regular occurrence for me in practice. Shooting is mostly mental, and I aspired toward a relaxed, practice-time attitude at all times. I would reel off sixty or seventy three-pointers in a row without thinking about it when I was shooting alone in a gym. That first round I didn't hear a sound, and I forgot anyone was watching. "The only shot that is important is the one that is in your hand," Tex Winter had taught us at Long Beach.

The second round I tied Dale Ellis from the Dallas Mavericks, fourteen to fourteen. After a twenty-four-second rematch against Dale, I felt fatigue setting in. I was naively confident entering the final round against Larry, who had easily beat Trent Tucker of the Knicks by five points in the semifinals. Larry demolished me in the final round, making nine straight shots, for a final score of twenty-two points to my measly twelve.

With his height advantage, Bird stood six inches closer to the basket than I did. He could use his set shot even from behind the three-point line. This helped him conserve energy in the later rounds, because he didn't have to jump to get the ball to the hoop. His technique simply required less motion. Launching all twenty-five shots in the sixty seconds allotted each round was a challenge, but Larry managed it with ease, never rushing his catapult-like, side-of-the-head shot form. In the end I was fated to become that second-place finisher he had goaded in the locker room.

The next year, in Seattle, I lost in the first round with only thirteen points. There was no excuse other than I couldn't find my touch. Larry, the only player who didn't bother to take off his warm-up jacket the entire competition, defeated Detlef Schrempf of the Indiana Pacers 16–14 for his second straight victory and the $12,500 prize. Detlef, unlike Larry, expended a lot of energy with his jump shot, and this hurt him as it had me the previous year.

In Chicago, in 1988, I lost again in the first round with only ten points, my worst round to date. I had anticipated this competition as a homecoming of sorts—my friends and family would be in the stands, and I was determined to impress them. In other words, I was far from the practice mind-set I strove for in competition. Again, Larry didn't bother to take off his warm-up jacket and still won, with seventeen points, over Dale Ellis. In my fourth three-point contest, in Houston, Larry sat out with a back problem. I thought I had the competition in the bag but lost to Ellis, who caught fire in the final round and won, nineteen to fifteen.

* * *

I'm a shooter. I never had to remind myself. Shooting baskets is as natural as walking to me. The thought of giving up on the competition, as frustrated as I'd felt losing year after year, never crossed my mind. The pain of losing was my motivator. I knew I'd eventually win. To accomplish that, however, I would need to rise above not just the competition but also the problems at home that were haunting me in the lead-up to the 1990 All-Star weekend.

After R. Kelly disappeared from our lives, Carlita began partying regularly with her sisters and old friends from high school, keeping up the late nights she'd grown accustomed to while helping Robert break into the music business. Many mornings she would stumble in while the kids and I ate breakfast, wearing the club clothes she'd left the house in the night before. I understood she was still seeking her own identity as well as a remedy for the abuse and neglect she had suffered as a child, and I tried to give her as much space as I could. I did everything to avoid conflict with her, worrying about the emotional toll a divorce would have on the kids. I also feared a divorce would be a costly disruption for me at that point in my career.

I stayed home nights when I wasn't on the road. Eventually, concerns about whether the kids were being properly taken care of while I was away began to outweigh the negative consequences of a divorce.

The breaking point between Carlita and me came one night in December. We'd said little in each other's company for months and were sleeping in separate rooms. Carlita woke me up in the middle of the night. "You hate me, don't you," she said, standing over me, ghost-like. The look in her eyes was vacant. A feeling of dread and an urge to take the kids as far as possible from that house overcame me. I sprang out of bed and started packing my clothes. She left the room without saying a word.

A few minutes later, as I carried my bags down the stairs and prepared to wake the kids, she pulled a knife from behind her back. "You've gone and lost your mind," I said, as I slowly backed up the stairs and then called 911. Carlita continued to stand there, blank-faced, at the bottom of the stairs. The police arrived and Carlita remained calm, too calm. The emptiness that filled her seemed to suck all the oxygen out of the house. The police suggested we sleep under separate roofs that night. The cops' advice jolted Carlita out of her trance, and sadness filled her eyes. She was lost. It was heartbreaking.

I filed for divorce a few days later and moved into an apartment with the kids. As much as it hurt, Carlita's partying, cheating, self-loathing, and emotional distance from me made any thoughts of reconciliation impossible.

Preoccupied with the divorce, I was preparing for the worst at that year's three-point competition in February. The three-point contest by then was the highlight of All-Star weekend for many, and Larry Bird was back. The 1990 contest featured the undisputed best shooters in the NBA: Reggie Miller, Craig Ehlo, Jon Sundvold, Mark Price, and Larry Bird. Michael Jordan also entered. Michael was far from the best three-point shooter in the league, but he believed he could win anything.

With Jordan and Bird in the competition, the spotlight was on the biggest names in the game—not on me, which worked in my favor. I faced off against Jordan in the first round, and the calm, practice mind-set I strove for set in. The buzzer sounded and we started shooting. The crowd was unusually boisterous for the initial round. *Was Jordan making all his shots?* I wondered. *This guy* does *win everything.* I blocked out the crowd and kept shooting. The final buzzer blared. I looked up at the scoreboard. Jordan only had five points, which still stands as the worst showing in three-point contest history. *This will be the last time we see Jordan in this contest,* I chuckled to myself.

The crowd couldn't believe Jordan missed so many shots either, which explains the howls from the stands. In spite of his drive to be the best at everything, Michael knew his limitations and would never again subject himself to such a low score; besides, it was bad for his brand. Larry Bird also unceremoniously exited the competition in the first round, and I felt a huge weight lift from my shoulders. The competition would be mine.

I scored twenty points the first round and seventeen in the second, which tied Jon Sundvold. My four previous losses strengthened my focus in overtime—I was stronger, not just physically but also mentally. I knew what I had to do and easily thumped Jon. In the final round matchup, I faced Reggie Miller, the legendary clutch shooter from the Pacers. I scored seventeen points against Reggie and finally accomplished one of my dreams as a professional basketball player.

Holding the gold trophy above my head, I thought of my Uncle Bruce, who taught me the "three Fs" of shooting: foundation, form, and follow-through. I thought of Tex Winter. I thought of the thousands of shots I had taken over the years and the endless tinkering, striving for the perfect shooting technique. My victory at All-Star weekend was a turning point in my career. It gave me the confidence and security to play on a championship team. From that moment I would have the full faith and credit of my teammates, I thought.

* * *

In high school I was a good shooter, my confidence stemming from the knowledge that I was better than most of the other players. Shooting was a feeling more than a formula for me in those years— I shot 60 percent from the field despite launching flat shots with little arc. In college, Tex's demonstration that two balls easily fit inside of the rim made a huge impression on me. "Don't ever tell me you are in a slump when you only have to shoot one ball and two fit in the rim," he said.

The two-ball trick triggered the realization that I was looking at the back of the rim as I shot, which meant I was looking under the rim. This explained why I missed short as often as I did. What I needed to do was to start looking over the rim. I raised my target by six inches. I began to visualize the point where the two balls met as Tex dropped them through the net. By aiming at that center point of the net, six inches up, I had room to breathe if I was off a few inches. Aiming higher meant I'd miss short less often and ensure I had the proper arc on my shot. The closer I was to the hoop, the more arc I needed. Farther away, the arc had to be flatter. Tex also cemented what Uncle Bruce had taught me about the importance of follow-through. "Don't break your follow-through until the ball is in the net," Tex said. That small detail developed my process and prompted me to visualize actually dropping the ball in the net from point-blank range, in a way.

Most players don't know why they make their shots; many rely on instinct. My goal was to understand why each shot I made went in. If I missed I would know exactly what needed to be corrected the next time. The most important revelation came during weekend practices on the farm in Walkerton, Indiana. I recognized there that I needed to keep the ball "cocked and locked" from the moment it touched my hands and maintain that as long as possible during the shooting process. Once my arms were fully extended, my wrist naturally moved into a follow-through, and I kept it there. There was no pushing with this method, only shooting. Every part of my body, from my feet to my hands, would be in rhythm until, as Tex said, "the shot goes through the net."

CHAPTER 14

WORKING TOGETHER

The Bulls attained the best record in franchise history, with sixty-one wins and twenty-one losses, in the 1990–91 season. The record topped the NBA that year and won us home court advantage through the playoffs. Throughout the season, an exultant momentum carried us onto the court. We scored 155 points against Phoenix one night in December, after scoring 151 just five games earlier in Denver. Scottie went sixteen for seventeen from the field in Charlotte in February. That year's All-Star weekend I won my second three-point contest, making a record nineteen consecutive shots—a personal victory for me, and another emotional boost for the team, which helped carry us into the season's second half. Knowing you have the league's three-point contest champion on your team is good for morale. Also, that season, Phil Jackson took some big risks, sitting Michael Jordan in the closing minutes of tight games. Phil wanted to prove to himself and the rest of us that we could win without Michael if need be. And we did.

One of the many things I love about sports, basketball in particular, is that it can remind us of what humans are capable of when they work together. A near-telepathic communication starts to form within the group. The isolation of being an individual lifts when a group works with respect toward the same end. The hard work in the gym, the triangle, the relentless defense, the leadership of Michael and Phil, and the unbreakable bond between the bench and the starters all combined to give us truly transcendent moments that season. We could feel ourselves transforming from a team that was building for the future to a team whose future was now.

Scottie Pippen gave me an encouraging pep talk before that year's three-point competition. "This is the boost we need, Hodge. Go out there and defend your title. Show the world we still have the best shooter in the league on our team." I picked up the first ball from the rack, and the feeling of peaceful detachment engulfed me. I hit shot after shot, round after round. Nothing else existed but the hoop, the ball, and me. I scored twenty points in the first round and sensed the competition was mine. Someone had to tell me after the semifinal round that I'd made nineteen in a row, for a total of twenty-four points. In the final round I scored seventeen points to beat Terry Porter. My combined score of sixty-one points was a new record for the highest combined score. I felt blissful afterward.

The league, however, would have preferred someone else won that year's three point championship, as Sam Smith notes in his book *The Jordan Rules:*

> Hodges's appearance as defending three point champion was being greeted with very little enthusiasm. League officials were worried that with the nation at war with a Muslim nation, Hodges might say something embarrassing if he won. There was talk of asking Hodges not to mention Allah in any postgame speech if he won.

The United States had begun bombing Iraq on January 17, 1991, two days after a US-mandated deadline for Iraq's withdrawal from Kuwait (January 15—Martin Luther King Jr.'s birthday). I knew Saddam Hussein was a former US ally and a vicious dictator who governed over a largely Muslim country. I didn't care what religion was most represented in Iraq. Like my coach, Phil Jackson, I believed that an imperial war, launched for the purpose of controlling other countries' resources and maintaining influence in a particular region, was a crime. The United States had no problem with Saddam the dictator, who kept his population under an iron thumb and did everything the United States asked of him under Reagan's watch during the Iran–Iraq war. I knew the Gulf War had nothing to do with liberating an oppressed people, as the media was spinning it. If I were going to speak out, I would speak out against a criminal act, not on behalf of Allah. Besides, if anyone had bothered to ask they would have known I didn't identify as Muslim.

Ever since my talk with Tom Enlund back in Phoenix, I knew the NBA higher-ups were scared of me. Grabbing a microphone at All-Star weekend was probably what they wanted me to do; it would be an excuse to run me out of the league. So I didn't give it to them. I would be more calculating and choose my battles to help ensure my longevity in the league, which would provide more opportunities to speak out against injustice.

I brought home the $20,000 prize money and my second gold trophy and was greeted with hearty cheers from the rest of the team back in Chicago. Winning the second three-point competition did more than advance my career; it helped create a little distance from a sad and confusing family situation, as my divorce with Carlita dragged out in court. Beyond politics, basketball was there for me when it felt like nothing else was. Basketball pulled me out of a dark place and helped me stay mindful—as Phil might say— and present for my kids. My connection to the game grew even deeper that weekend. I never felt more grateful to be a professional basketball player in the NBA.

Soon after All-Star weekend, Phil Jackson asked the entire team in a practice before a game against Milwaukee, "Who wants the troops to go into Baghdad and go after Hussein?" Pippen's, Grant's, and Jordan's hands went up, as did those of most of the other players in the locker room. Jordan, whose brother was in the army and stationed in Germany at the time, said, "We should bomb the shit out of that motherfucker." There was a chorus of cheers from the rest of the players.

It felt like Phil and I were the only ones in that room who recognized the inhumanity, injustice, and stupidity of it all. Phil responded, "Don't you all realize there will be blowback? Do you think you can incite violence on people and have no repercussions? Do you really want your son blown up in some movie theater because we made Iraq a terrorist nation? The repercussions of this war will affect generations to come. . . . It will further compromise our freedoms here at home, too." Phil was predicting, before just about anyone else that I knew of, the post-9/11 national security state that would be built up as part of the Global War on Terror.

As Phil spoke, Martin Luther King Jr.'s speech, "Beyond Vietnam," echoed in my mind. A little more than a month prior, I had reread the speech after a ceremony in Atlanta. Michael Jordan had called my hotel room hours before the event and said, "Hey, Hodge, do you want to fill in for me at this MLK wreath ceremony?" He and Dominique Wilkins had been invited to join Coretta Scott King in laying a wreath on King's grave in a formal observance of his birthday, which coincided with our road trip to Atlanta. "This is your thing, not mine, Hodge," said Jordan.

Dominique and I placed the wreath on King's grave, which rests alongside that of his mother, Alberta Williams King, who was gunned down in 1974 in Ebenezer Baptist Church. The marble graves sit atop an elevated circle of Georgia red clay bricks, surrounded by a reflecting pool. The experience was beyond moving. I had never felt more connected to my mom and aunts, who had struggled and organized alongside King in the '60s.

Phil Jackson, Bill Cartwright, and I met with Coretta in a private room of the gravesite museum after the ceremony. The media and Coretta's handlers were kept out. Coretta turned to me and asked, "Craig do you realize how painful it is for me to have the people who are responsible for Martin's death pay for this museum? Hypocrisy and cover-up stare me in the face every time I come here." She continued on about the Gulf War and how upset she was that the US government had chosen January 15, Martin's birthday, as a deadline to start the bombing. "I can't think of a greater insult to Martin's memory, and it just adds salt to the wound knowing that so many Black men and women will die in disproportionate numbers fighting the war."

After the meeting I went to the library and reread the speech I had last read at Long Beach State:

> We are called to speak for the weak, for the voiceless, for the victims of our nation and for those it calls "enemy," for no document from human hands can make these humans any less our brothers. . . . One day we must come to see that the whole Jericho Road must be transformed so that men and women will not be constantly beaten and robbed as they make their journey on life's highway. True compassion is more than flinging a coin to a beggar. It comes to see that an edifice which produces beggars needs restructuring. . . . A true revolution of values will lay hands on the world order and say of war, "This way of settling differences is not just." This business of burning human beings with napalm, of filling our nation's homes with orphans and widows, of injecting poisonous drugs of hate into the veins of peoples normally humane, of sending men home from dark and bloody battlefields physically handicapped and psychologically deranged, cannot be reconciled with wisdom, justice, and love. A nation that continues year after year to spend more money on military defense than on programs of social uplift is approaching spiritual death.

I thought of the other players, our stars: Jordan, Pippen, Grant. None of these brothers knew Black history. Here were some of the most influential Black men in America—and they were blind to the impact US foreign policy had around the world. The words of one of our greatest Black leaders were foreign to them.

Later that year, in a bus heading to Milwaukee, I was talking to a group of guys about the importance of education, in particular about Black history. "What do I need education for? I make six figures," said Scottie. I shook my head, concealing my frustration, and said, "Well, you know that wealth means nothing if your kids, family, and neighbors don't know our history. Any one of us could be shot dead for simply walking in the wrong neighborhood at the wrong time." There was little disagreement but I could see my words weren't penetrating beyond the surface.

I don't bring this up to shame Scottie, Michael, and other players who aren't educated in our history. I bring it up because we can't solve a problem if we don't recognize the sickness. Michael didn't speak out largely because he didn't know what to say, not because he was a bad person. When we were about to win our first championship against the Lakers, Jordan said, "I'm not going to the White House. Fuck Bush. I didn't vote for him." And, true to his word, he didn't go. Jordan was full of contradictions, rooted in a political ignorance that wasn't necessarily his fault.

It was reassuring, though, that Phil Jackson was in my corner. Although not terribly outspoken with his own politics beyond the occasional locker room discussion, Phil helped inspire me to use my platform to speak out, and not to be overly discouraged by my teammates' lack of political will. Phil was one of the smartest, most thoughtful people I knew. When the smart guy is on your side it emboldens you. It was never a "Black versus white" thing with me. If you recognized injustice and fought it, even in quiet ways, as Phil did, you were all right in my book.

* * *

The Bulls opened the Eastern Conference finals at home that year against the two-time defending Detroit champions. We were anxious to meet our nemesis again. In another tight game we found ourselves up by only three points to start the fourth quarter. Recognizing that Detroit played their best basketball in the final minutes, Phil had grown accustomed to resting Michael, Horace, and Scottie at the beginning of the fourth against Detroit in the regular season. Even in this close, critical playoff game Phil stuck to his game plan.

B. J. Armstrong, Cliff Levingston, Will Perdue, and I led the team onto the court while Jordan and Pippen sat. This was a crucial moment. Detroit could have bounced back and broken open a big lead. Their starters stayed on the floor. Phil was demonstrating trust in his bench when it mattered most. We increased the lead from three to nine. Michael, Scottie, and Horace reentered the game with the score 81–72. If there were any question about the depth of our bench or whether this was only Michael's team, it was erased that quarter. We held onto the lead and won 94–83.

In the final game of the Detroit series, Dennis Rodman threw Scottie Pippen a few rows into the stands. In previous years such a brazen act of aggression from Detroit would have caused a bench-clearing brawl. But this episode showed further evidence of how far we had come as a team. Rather than charging back at Rodman with fists flying, Scottie emerged from the stands Buddha-faced, and proceeded to sink two free throws. Rodman fumed. Pippen—and our team—didn't take the bait. Our team chemistry was maintained. The hard work in the gym, the seriousness with which we played in practice, and our newfound ability to not unravel into hostile individuals in tense moments finally allowed us to neutralize Detroit.

With seven seconds on the clock, as our four-game sweep was about to come to pass, Detroit's starters, with the exception of Joe Dumars, walked off the court. Past our bench, glaring at us from the

corners of their eyes, the Pistons offered no handshake or congratula-
tions. No other team in playoff history had left the court early that
way. The Bad Boys hated us. The walk-off was a "fuck you" to Michael
and Scottie, who were the most vocal in postgame press conferences
about Detroit's dirty play. The press feigned outrage but secretly
loved the drama. Many criticized the self-proclaimed Bad Boys as
unsportsmanlike losers with no honor or respect for basketball.

As for me, I thought the gesture was fitting. Detroit stayed true
to the image they had created for themselves. Anything less than
rude, obnoxious, we-don't-give-a-shit-what-you-think behavior on
their part would have tainted the manner in which they had won
their previous two championships. I respected them for not breaking stride in defeat. The Pistons left everything they had on the
court and exited the stage of basketball history in the same manner
that they played.

Now we had to face the team in purple and gold from Los
Angeles. The Lakers had beaten Clyde Drexler, Terry Porter, and
Jerome Kersey of the Portland Trail Blazers in the Western Conference finals, four games to two. It was our turn to face Magic
Johnson (by this point a five-time NBA champion), James Worthy,
and Byron Scott in the finals. As much as I was looking forward
to playing in my first NBA championship, I couldn't shake the image of John Carlos and Tommie Smith on the podium, with their
Black Power fists outstretched, at the 1968 Olympics in Mexico
City. *What would I do on basketball's biggest stage?* I asked myself. I
felt I owed it to the next generation to make the most of my moment standing before the world.

At that point in my career I had no illusions that we were playing "just a game." Too much money was at stake. Too many eyes
were tuned in. As Isiah's fall from grace after he spoke up about
race proved, too much needed to be suppressed in order to allow
the "game" to function as the billion-dollar industry it had become.

Magic Johnson and Larry Bird, after their famous duel in the NCAA finals in 1979, helped fuel the individual endorsement windfall, which in many ways swallowed up politically outspoken high-profile players. If the top players wanted to keep the income they were receiving in endorsements, they had to fall in line with the demands of their sponsors, which usually meant silently smiling their way through their professional life. Owners also expected players not to offend the league's corporate sponsors. Black men in the NBA had to keep quiet in front of a national audience if they wanted to keep their money.

I was determined to do my part to change this. I missed the Bill Russells, Oscar Robertsons, and Kareems of the league. Like them, I wanted to stay true to my conscience and the obligation I felt to my family, my professors, and the Black community as a whole by taking advantage of my opportunity on the great NBA stage to speak truth to power.

I had been formulating an idea that would draw on lessons of the past, an idea with precedent, and an idea that would make waves around the world if seen through. Back in 1964, the NBA Players' Association had demanded a pension plan, trainers, meal money, and treatment as partners in the business instead of as disposable equipment. The owners ignored the requests for years. Finally, the players had enough.

Led by Oscar Robertson, Tom Heinsohn, Jerry West, and Elgin Baylor, the biggest stars threatened to boycott the very first televised All-Star game. They actually showed up to the stadium and told the owners they weren't stepping on the court to play the game unless the union's demands were met on the spot. Lakers owner Bob Short tried to break into the locker room, where the players were huddled, to demand an end to the holdout. Stopped by a guard at the door, Short said, "Tell Elgin Baylor if he doesn't get his ass out here fast I'm done with him."

Word drifted back to Baylor, who replied, "Tell Bob Short to go fuck himself."[10] After more threats by the owners, who were feeling the pressure from ABC-TV executives about to pull the plug on the game, the owners finally agreed to all of the players' demands. The players withheld their labor at precisely the right time and won a victory for every NBA player to follow.

I felt like we owed it to those guys to continue the fight. Yes, times were different. In the early '60s, NBA players had to work summer jobs; in 1991 the average annual salary was $865,000. For many, there was a lot to lose: a dream job, financial security, adoring fans, and much more. Yet a united front presented by the two teams vying for an NBA championship could wield enormous power. We would stand in solidarity with the Black community while calling out racism and economic inequality in the NBA, where there were no Black owners and almost no Black coaches despite the fact that 75 percent of the players in the league were African American. We could also be a powerful example to other unions if we could remind the rest of the country of the power of withholding labor. And we couldn't forget that modern-day players would be nothing if it weren't for the sacrifices of players who fought in the sixties. Imagine it: a united front before all those people watching at home and in the Madhouse on Madison.

Before game one, in warm-ups, I pulled Michael Jordan to the side and told him that I thought he and I should encourage our players to boycott the game. I cited the action at the 1964 All-Star game. I said we could wait for everyone to fill the stadium, the cameras would begin to roll, and then we would stand in opposition to racism and economic inequality both in the Black community and in the NBA. I knew if I could get Michael on board the rest of the team would follow. We were a tight unit. Michael said I was crazy and quickly dismissed my idea.

Disappointed but undeterred, I approached Magic Johnson during warm-ups and said the same thing to him, knowing he would have the same kind of influence in the Lakers locker room. "That's too extreme, man," said Magic.

"What's happening to our people in this country is extreme," I replied. "We need to take advantage of this moment." All-Star weekend and the playoffs are when the owners make all their money, but they couldn't make a dime if we refused to play. This wasn't the first time Magic and Michael had heard such talk from me. Everyone in the league knew they were eventually going to get an earful of political talk if they bumped into me. Many players tended to agree with my words and generally supported the idea that more had to be done to structurally change the way Black people were treated in America. It was time for action. Maybe we didn't need Michael and Magic, but it was hard to ignore the influence both had with their respective teams.

✳ ✳ ✳

The game started according to schedule. After the jump ball, I pushed thoughts of the boycott into the back of my head and focused on the task at hand. Against the Lakers we wanted 70 percent of our points to come off of the fast break. The idea was always to run on numbers. We wanted more of our guys to get down the court on offense before their guys had a chance to set up and defend their goal. If we didn't have the numbers we'd flow into triangle. In the triangle we wanted to pass a lot and use dribble entry with Michael and Scottie—if they had the ball they would drive, if their shots weren't available they would kick it out to the shooters. In the final minutes of each game the rule was absolutely no turnovers. *If I can't see your numbers, I'm not passing the ball.* "Never make a marginal pass," Phil would tell us.

We were nervous that first game. The Lakers had been to the finals five times in the previous decade. They used their experience and composure to beat us 93–91, after a clutch three-pointer by Sam Perkins with fourteen seconds on the clock and a couple of missed free throws from Jordan.

After the loss, the tone in the locker room was serious. We knew this was our series to lose. Our play throughout the year showed that the 1991 Lakers could not stop us if we stayed in our lanes, remembered our roles within the team, and conserved energy where possible. Previous years had taught us how much of a toll an eighty-two-game season and an extended playoff series can have on the body, so Phil used the word "steady" a lot. There would be no wasted energy.

Before game two, Scottie announced that the rest of the team shouldn't expect much from him offensively, but he was going to give Magic hell all game long. We walked out on the floor at Chicago Stadium to deafening noise. The crowd was rowdy—the fans had shaken their jitters from the first game, so now it was up to us to shake ours. Horace Grant's ten points in the first quarter gave us back the self-confidence that had carried us all season. We could have gone off track in the third quarter when Michael was forced to sit due to foul trouble, but the rest of the team, driven by Phil's confidence-building techniques, stepped up and scored thirty-eight points that quarter. When Jordan returned he went on his own run, with thirteen straight baskets that were topped off by his famous right-to-left midair switch-of-the-hands shot as he drove to the hoop against Sam Perkins. True to his word, Pippen held Magic to only fourteen points. We won by twenty-one that game and knew the tide had shifted.

* * *

The Great Western Forum, the site of game three, was twenty miles north of Long Beach State and twenty miles south of where Rodney King had been beaten only three months prior by the LAPD. I had seen the horrifying tape of the officers dealing the eleven fractures to King while he was incapacitated on the ground. Reminded of my friend Ron Settles and his death in police custody while I was at Long Beach, I knew such beatings were standard operating procedure and that police were never held accountable for these abuses of power. This seemed different, though, because it was caught on tape. I thought the evidence against the officers was too damning, and justice would be served.

While I was in Los Angeles, NFL legend and civil rights icon Jim Brown asked me if I would invite everyone on the Bulls over to his house in the West Hollywood Hills. Jim knew I was volunteering with the Amer-I-Can program in Chicago, an organization he'd founded in 1988 to give children at risk of joining gangs help with school and leadership skills. At the time of the playoffs, Jim was trying to negotiate a truce between rival LA gangs the Crips and the Bloods, and he wanted the support and input of the Bulls. I explained this to the team but quickly saw that I was the only one interested in the meeting. "I want to stay focused on the series, but ask Jim how he made all his money," Jordan said.

I couldn't wait to go to Jim's house. My taxi pulled up to a beautiful home way up in the hills. My palms were sweating. I'd met a lot of famous people by that point in my career, but this was the first time I remember feeling nervous about it. Jim's front door was wide open, so I walked into an empty, plush living room.

"Mr. Brown?" I called out sheepishly. I noticed sliding-glass doors that led out to a pool. There, Jim was waving me over to the pool area. He was sitting with T. Rodgers, one of the notorious cofounders of the Bloods. Rodgers, a product of Chicago's South Side and a former member of the Blackstone Rangers, was at this time trying to make it as a Hollywood actor. Both T. Rodgers and Jim received me with warmth. We sat by the pool and looked out over the Los Angeles skyline. The view was striking.

After a little chitchat, Jim got right to it. "So Craig, do you consider yourself a member of the Nation of Islam?" Surprised by his directness and the seriousness of his tone, I knew my answer would determine the dynamic of our relationship. I was aware that he was very friendly with Minister Farrakhan and had been for some time. But I went with the truth.

"No, Jim. I'm not. I'm a sympathizer, and I attend the minister's services from time to time, but I've never officially been a member of the organization."

Jim sat there for a second, his hands pressed together in contemplation. "Good. What Farrakhan does is for Farrakhan. You are bigger than one organization. You'd be pigeonholing yourself if you limited yourself to the Nation."

The mood lightened and we talked about the movie project T. Rodgers and Jim were working on together. Then we spoke about the Crips and the Bloods. I knew the gangs' history from my studies with Dr. Karenga, but listening to T. Rodgers's perspective was fascinating. Brown and Rodgers both believed that if members of the rival gangs understood their own history better they would find it easier to reconcile. We talked about the rise of the BPP and Dr. Karenga's Us organization, the contributions they made to the Black liberation movement, and the FBI's calculated efforts to destroy them through COINTELPRO.

Initially, the Bloods and the Crips had tried to carry on the mission of the Panthers and Us to strengthen and protect the community, and to give young people a sense of pride and purpose. But their leadership, as I learned from talking with Jim and T. Rodgers, wasn't strong enough, and, eventually, the Crips and Bloods turned inward and began targeting each other with relentless violence. Brown and Rodgers wanted to do their part to change this by helping to fill the leadership vacuum. The wounds were so deep, though, and the rivalry so entrenched, that we could do little more than discuss the issues at that point.

Gun violence, of course, was a major subject. When the talk turned to our personal experiences, I noted that I'd had only a few run-ins with guns in my youth, but they were enough to turn me off guns completely. There was the terrifying time at King courts when an offended ballplayer came back with a weapon and started shooting. Another near brush with violence took place in our home, when I was just a little kid. My Aunt Jeri was washing dishes, my mom was reading, and I stared at the TV from the floor. A neighbor named Charles Barnett opened our unlocked front door and walked into the living room, slurring his speech and holding a sawed-off shotgun.

My mom, who was sometimes known to be a little high-strung, took control of the moment with a stone face. She zeroed in on Charles's eyes and called me toward her. When I was within arms' reach she pulled me behind her with a steady hand and said to Charles, "You need to leave this house, now." My mom seemed to will the man out of the house with her calm, assured voice and sharp eyes. When Charles was almost out, my uncles came up from behind and jumped on him. My mom, Aunt Jeri, and I left through the back door. That was the last time we were ever bothered by Charles.

The only other gun incident I could recall was when I once shot a bird through the eye with a BB gun. The brown bird fell from the branch it was on and landed in front of my feet. I stared at it. A nervous tingle ran through my shoulders and legs. Then a hollow feeling settled into my chest. I thought of the bird's family and how sad they would be. I then thought about my own granddad as I started walking home at a quick pace. Tears started pouring down my face as I imagined the same thing happening to him. That was the last time I touched a gun.

Jim, T. Rodgers, and I talked well into the night and agreed to resume at a future date. As we shared our ideas and experiences, I thought of my teammates and how much they could have benefited from—and contributed to—the discussion. Of course, we were in LA on a mission, yet I held fast to my belief that there was room for more than one.

* * *

The Lakers managed to amass a thirteen-point lead over us in the third quarter of game three, but we came roaring back with a 20–7 fourth quarter. With ten seconds left on the clock, Vlade Divac nailed two free throws after being fouled following an entry pass—almost stolen by Horace Grant—from Magic Johnson, to put the Lakers up two. The next play, after calling a time out, Phil Jackson decided we should inbound the ball under the Lakers' basket. Normally a team would opt to take the ball out at midcourt, but Phil wanted Michael to generate a full head of steam by running the length of the floor, which he hoped would catch the Lakers off guard.

Michael pulled up for a clutch jumper just inside the paint with seven-foot-one Divac's giant hand squarely in Jordan's face, with seven seconds to go. We went into overtime, where Jordan scored six of our twelve points. "Good News" Cliff Levingston, our six-foot-eight power forward, came fresh-legged off the bench to shoot down Magic's efforts to ignite the Lakers' offense. Jordan scored two acrobatic baskets in those final minutes of game three, but it was Levingston's defense against Magic Johnson that made the difference for us. We won game three 104–96, our first playoffs victory in the Great Western Forum.

In game four the Lakers took a first-quarter lead and lost it in the second, never to regain it. James Worthy and Byron Scott were hampered by injuries, and the Lakers couldn't get back into a shooting groove. Jordan played with a jammed toe but still managed twenty-eight points and thirteen assists. John Paxson went seven for eleven from the field for fifteen points. His shot rarely touched the rim—it was a thing of beauty. The Lakers were battered, bruised, and tired. We went into game five knowing the championship was ours.

Game five was tight, in spite of Worthy and Scott being side-lined. Magic Johnson had a dazzling twenty-assist game and re-fused to let us win easily. Scottie lit up the scoreboard with thirty-two points, but it wasn't until John Paxson scored ten points in the final minutes of the fourth quarter that we knew we had won.

In the locker room we were up to our eyeballs in champagne. Michael hugged the trophy and cried with his father, James. My friends from Long Beach joined me for the all-night party in the hotel. We would be greeted by a ticker-tape parade in Chicago. From King courts to Bloom to Rich East to Long Beach to the Clippers, Bucks, and finally the Bulls, I had climbed the highest athletic mountaintop to reach the pinnacle of the basketball world. I was a world champion, and I had done it with my hometown team. I only had one more year on my contract, and I knew if I continued to play like I had been, I could name my price as a free agent. But even with all the bliss I was feeling, it was incomplete. I couldn't help thinking that I'd had a national platform and didn't use it to help my people. I should have worked harder to get the others to join me in a boycott. I couldn't stop imagining what might have been—if we had not walked on the court that first game of the series, and instead fought for a different type of victory.

CHAPTER 15

IN SEARCH OF A DYNASTY

Not content to let us rest on our laurels, Phil made sure our training camp before the 1991–92 season was competitive and serious. We knew all the teams in the league would be gunning for our championship trophy, so we placed a lot of pressure on ourselves to match the intensity of the opposing team each night. Phil wanted us not just to maintain our level of play but also to exceed expectations of ourselves. Tex and Phil tasked me with making sure Scottie and Horace, who had often expressed concerns about not being fully plugged into the triangle offense, both understood its finer points. Having run the triangle since college, I knew the offense as well as Tex did at that point. I spent hours teaching Scottie and Horace how to roll off screens and step into pockets where they could receive entry passes or find players cutting for easy assists. I never felt more valuable to a team than I did with the Bulls that year, like a de facto assistant coach. Every practice, I wasn't just playing. I was teaching.

Like the Lakers and the Celtics, we were striving for dynastic rule in the league. We aspired to be historically great. That season, we were on fire right out of the gate, winning fourteen of our first seventeen games. Phil emphasized winning streaks and small team goals that could break the season down into more immediate and manageable units. Michael "only" averaged thirty points a game that season and consciously worked on filling in the blanks wherever there was an opportunity. Scottie was now—if he hadn't been in years past—fully integrated into the offense. He scored his first forty-point game in February against the Bucks and began to show the signs that he would one day join Michael in the NBA Hall of Fame. Horace Grant embraced his role as the team's workhorse, scrapping for every loose ball and rebound.

Bill Cartwright continued to thwart the likes of Hakeem Olajuwon, Patrick Ewing, and David Robinson in the paint; Cliff Levingston, B. J. Armstrong, Will Perdue, and others provided depth off the bench. I proved myself on the court on plenty of occasions, such as the time I scored twenty-one points against the Phoenix Suns the night Michael Jordan was suspended for "intentionally" making physical contact with referee Tommie Wood in a triple overtime loss against Utah in the previous game.[11]

Again, however, my personal life threatened to overshadow my enjoyment of success on the court. Less than a week before Christmas 1991, my private life would become national news. From the *New York Times* to the *Chicago Tribune* the headlines were similar: "Hodges's Wife Arrested, Charged With Aggravated Battery."

The court had given me temporary custody of the kids as the divorce proceedings with Carlita dragged on. She saw the boys on weekends and holidays, and in the beginning the arrangement seemed to work. She and I spoke on the phone to coordinate visits but not much more beyond that.

My cousins Jason and Rodney, who were in college at Southern Illinois University and were staying at my house over their Christmas break, helped me get the kids to school the morning of December 19, 1991. We were all excited because it was one of the last days of school before the kids' holiday vacation started. Jason, Rodney, Jamaal, and I sat in the car, waiting for the morning bell to ring at Jamaal's school in Northbrook, the Chicago suburb where we lived. We'd already dropped off Jibril.

Jamaal noticed Carlita's car. "Look, Dad, Mom's here," he said nervously, knowing she was breaking with visitation protocol. Carlita walked up to the window on the passenger's side, where I was sitting, and knocked gently on the window with her leather gloves. I rolled the window down, ignoring my instinct to keep it up. Maybe there was some type of emergency, I thought.

Carlita poked her head in and looked at Jamaal, who was about seven at the time, sitting in the back seat. Her look was apologetic. Then she turned to me and screamed, "Are you ready to die, motherfucker?" As she yelled she doused me with what looked like water from a Snapple bottle. My work jacket was soaked. I started laughing out of disbelief, not knowing what to make of it. As I laughed she tried to light matches and flick them at me. The weather was bitterly cold and somewhat windy, so none of the matches would light. Probably not wanting to accept what was happening—I still hadn't processed that she had poured gasoline on me—I opened the car door. As Carlita continued to threaten to kill me, I ushered Jamaal out of the car, past her, and into the school.

It wasn't until I walked through the first of the school's set of double doors, where the collision of temperatures swirled the air enough to carry the smell of gasoline to my nose, that I realized what she had tried to do. The gravity of the situation hit me like a sucker punch. I told the school secretary, sitting at a desk near the door, "This is going to sound crazy, but I think my wife just tried to light me on fire."

Carlita had fled the scene by the time the police arrived. Jamaal was shaken but was too young to comprehend what had happened—at least that has been his story since that day. The police found Carlita in her apartment, arrested her in the fur coat she had been wearing, and booked her on assault charges. She spent the night in prison and posted bond. I filed a restraining order. She didn't need prison as much as she needed psychiatric help, so I didn't press charges.

When I woke up the next morning and saw the headlines, my immediate concern was the kids. The divorce proceedings had been traumatizing enough for them; now this. My mom and my aunts, Jason, and Rodney helped provide emotional support and stability for our household in the days and weeks after the event. The thought of going back on the road troubled me, but I didn't have much choice if I wanted to keep my job with the Bulls. My family assured me they would maintain a vigilant watch for Carlita and make sure she kept her distance from our children. There was no telling what she was capable of now.

* * *

The Bulls weren't thrilled with this distraction amid our run for a second championship, but I played it off like a freak occurrence and assured Phil that the incident wasn't going to interfere with my play on the court. Soon the jokes started rolling in. Arsenio Hall mentioned the incident in the opening monologue of his late-night show. Horace and Scottie, when I would get into a solid shooting groove, would say, "Watch out, our boy Hodge is on fire!" I certainly wasn't the only one with marital issues—mine just happened to be the most public and dramatic.

In truth I was embarrassed, not just for the kids and myself but also for Carlita. Knowing there wasn't anything I could do for her made me deeply sad. She and I had lived through a lot together. She will always be the mother of my children. I loved her. My job, my travel, my instinct to bury my feelings in difficult situations triggered pain in her. The best thing I could do was keep my distance. I dug deep and threw myself into basketball and activism. Hard work, leadership, and compassion on and off the court became my focus. As I said to a reporter at the time, regarding all the attention, "I look at it like a trial. It's like I've gotten all these gifts, and the test is to see what I'm doing with them." I felt challenged yet grateful. Now I had to stay busy.

I threw myself into an organization I founded with Queen Latifah, Chuck D, and Sister Souljah called Operation UNITE—Save the Youth. UNITE grew out of my frustrations with the inequalities I saw in the schools across the Chicagoland area. Our organization initiated exchange programs between the highest funded, predominantly white schools in and around Chicago and the poorest Black schools. The hope was for inner-city Black kids to understand that a better world was possible and to be inspired to fight for better conditions for themselves. I also knew kids in low-income schools didn't receive the social and psychological help they needed to deal with the effects of poverty, so I encouraged kids in UNITE to form leadership councils, not just to talk about ways to improve the community but also to serve as support networks—an alternative to gangs, you might say.

I called it "Operation" because the body of the Black community needed a direct intervention. My motto for the organization was that change only occurs when there is unity—when people UNITE. I wanted players in the league to start accepting responsibility for their communities, too, so I hit up everyone I knew for support, and not just financial support but mentorship. The response was mixed. Again, players like Horace and Scottie were enthusiastic in initial conversations. The problem was follow-through.

✳ ✳ ✳

The sound of tanned leather whistling through the cotton-white net was the only noise, at least for me, in the sold-out Amway Arena in Orlando. It was February 1992, the final round of the three-point contest at All-Star weekend.

The clock is running down. I reach for the next twenty-two-ounce ball resting on the metal rack. My body feels like it is on autopilot: the right wrist cocks, feet fall in shoulder-width apart, eyes zero in two inches above the center of the hoop, right elbow tucks tight into my torso as I jump from the perfectly planed hardwood. It's almost like I'm watching the whole thing from above. The basketball rises through the middle of my chin and over my head, arms extend fully, the ball rolls off my spread fingers upon release, and my palm collapses in the follow-through. My white-and-red LA Gear shoes—believe me, they were fresh in the early '90s—come back to the floor. There is an instant of silence . . . I hear the swish.

In fluid, rapid, regular succession the NBA-emblazoned basketballs soar high above the red, pronged, metal rim to peak and fall at the exact height. Good arc optimizes the size of the target. My math is correct every time, but I don't think about it. My body understands the equation deep below my skin. Starting at twenty-two feet from the post in the corner of the court, and increasing to twenty-three feet, nine inches, at the farthest of the five racks, I shuttle around the perimeter. The number of made shots creeps higher, but I'm not counting. There are no past or future shots; there is only the one I'm shooting in that moment.

Next up was Jim Les, a point guard from the Sacramento Kings. For a moment I thought he would win. He almost beat me with the red-white-and-blue double-point money ball on the final shot, but he didn't. I scored sixteen of a possible thirty points in the final round, winning my third straight three-point contest that weekend. The only other person to win three straight was the legendary Larry Bird. ("Who's comin' in second?")

All I could hear was the applause of the crowd. I held the large gold basketball trophy high above my head, wearing a black nylon jacket with the words "UNITE" in gold letters on the front. Wearing the jacket broke with uniform protocol, but I didn't care. I was on top of the world, so why not help save it? Flavor Flav, Chuck D, and Queen Latifah were also wearing their UNITE jackets. We were on a mission. I felt taller than the highest point in the stadium.

I was interviewed by NBC with Jibril by my side after the competition. The reporter asked Jibril, "What do you think of your Dad winning the competition?"

"I thought that white dude was gonna beat my Daddy," said Jibril. My young revolutionary made the most of his moment on the national stage.

On the bus back to the hotel, Curly Neal, who played twenty-two seasons with the Harlem Globetrotters, was sitting by himself in the back row. The last time I'd seen Curly was my sophomore year at Long Beach. I considered Curly one of the most gifted ballhandlers in the world, as did just about everyone else.

"You were worried, weren't you?" he asked, as I walked down the aisle with Jibril.

"Nah."

"He had ten balls left. He needed to make six. How many did he make?"

"Five."

"As he was shooting his last ball, you know what I did?" Curly asked, with a proud, mysterious look on his face.

"What, Curly?"

"I blew in the air." He smiled and winked.

Jibril was eager to get back to the hotel. He was in the middle of an epic, weekend-long one-on-one game with the son of another three-point contestant—Steph, the son of Dell Curry.

✳ ✳ ✳

Back in Chicago, Scottie Pippen, Horace Grant, B. J. Armstrong, Michael Jordan, and I were sitting in cushy white chairs in the home locker room in Chicago Stadium before a game. We were on track to win our second straight NBA championship. A mail courier arrived and handed me a white envelope. I tore it open and looked down to see the $20,000 three-point-contest prize money. That check equaled half my annual salary when I entered the league in 1982.

I stared at the green bank paper for a minute. I wasn't the richest person in the room by a long shot, but I was comfortable. I lived in a safe house on Chicago's North Shore. Financially, I had come a long way since my days in the poor and segregated neighborhood of Chicago Heights. I stood up and walked to the center of the room, where I dropped the check and watched it flutter to the floor.

"Who's with me?" I asked. Everyone stared, silent. "What are we going to do?" I continued. Right outside the stadium doors, on the West Side of one of the largest cities in the country, you could see it: the poverty, the inequality, the pain. The plight of Black people in the United States had called to me my whole life. Now I was in a position to make a lasting difference. So was every player in that room.

"What do you want to do, Hodge?" someone asked.

We could make a commercial, buy a few billboards. We could hold a press conference amid the blight, with the community behind us. Even better, we could help bring jobs to our community, I explained. Phil Knight, the CEO of Nike, was paying pennies on the dollar to laborers in Southeast Asia to manufacture the shoes we were all wearing. Shoes that kids were killing each other over in the streets. Why not let the community buying these products produce them? They could share in the profits. This was my plan. We could pool our money and start something in the communities that had raised us. B. J. Armstrong was from Detroit, Michigan; Scottie Pippen was from Hamburg, Arkansas; Horace Grant was from Macon, Georgia; Michael Jordan was from Wilmington, North Carolina. We could set up factories in all those towns.

"I hear where you're coming from, Hodge, but I gotta talk to my guy first," was the prevailing, polite, indifferent response in the locker room.

Sure, we all had our private charities that our accountants and financial advisors set up for us, with tax benefits. But we were winning championships together. We didn't need to consult our guys, did we? Besides, these accountants and finance guys had no direct interest in the betterment of the Black community. Of course they would discourage this type of action. But why was there such a reflex to ask for permission in the first place? Well, I knew the answer, but I was still disappointed. I'd learned from my studies and experience that Black people, even the wealthiest among us, have been conditioned to wait for the white man to sign off on our movements.

I envisioned the Chicago Bulls making history in the most meaningful way possible. We were more than just athletes if we wanted to be. We could be freedom fighters, too, on the front lines of the second civil rights movement in the United States, fighting for justice. We also happened to have a basketball player whose popularity exceeded that of the Pope. If the Bulls spoke in a collective voice, during the golden age of professional basketball, the world would listen.

CHAPTER 16

PLAYING THE GAME

The Bulls steamrolled over all comers in the regular 1991–1992 season. We clinched home court advantage for the playoffs, exceeding our sixty-one wins of the previous year with sixty-seven, the fourth-best finish in NBA history. Sportswriters predicted smooth sailing for us through the playoffs. But because teams threw everything they had at us, it felt like each night of the regular season was a playoff game. This took a toll. Preserving our energy with steady play continued to be a priority.

The opening round against the Miami Heat was a three-game sweep. On April 29, the third and final game of the series, Jordan scored fifty-six points. April 29, 1992, was also the day all charges were dismissed against the four LAPD officers accused in the beating of Rodney King and the subsequent cover-up. That night, riots broke out in Los Angeles.

I tried not to let the events in LA distract me, but I felt too close to the situation to ignore it. Many people were dismissing the rioters as looters and thugs. This ignored not only the horrifying injustice of the verdict but also the decades of militarized oppression by law enforcement in Black communities. It was all I could do to bite my tongue. If I'd had my way, the '92 playoffs would have been boycotted until justice was served in the King case. And I felt somewhat alone in that conviction. Somebody asked MJ what he thought about the Rodney King verdict, and Jordan replied, "I need to know more about it."

Following the sweep against the Heat, we were off to face John Starks, Patrick Ewing, Pat Riley, and the New York Knicks in the second round. The Knicks came out swinging, playing dirty and showing us their best basketball of the year. Their intensity, reminiscent of the Detroit Bad Boys' play the previous year, took us by surprise. Led by Xavier McDaniel, New York tried to unnerve us as a team and cause us to play as heated, separate individuals. Once again, Scottie, McDaniel's main target, had to do everything in his power to contain his emotions against flagrant foul after flagrant foul. There were a few shoving matches between the two, but, overall, Scottie and the rest of the team managed to keep cool.

The Knicks forced seven games. Cliff Levingston led us onto the court for the deciding game with his ritualistic locker room howl, "What time is it?!?!" We responded with a raucous "Game Time!" We beat the Knicks by twenty and proved to ourselves and the rest of the world how strong our character was. Pressed up against the wall, we showed we could win when it mattered most.

When we weren't on the court, though, I was glued to the TV, watching events unfold during the six-day riots in LA, which would inflict a billion dollars' worth of damages on the city, leaving fifty-five dead and more than two thousand injured.

I still resisted the urge to speak out as we prepared to meet the Cleveland Cavaliers. The Cavs were eager to avenge the 1989 series, when Jordan's otherworldly shot had knocked them out of the playoffs. Gatorade had been running the "Be Like Mike" ad campaign, featuring "The Shot," for almost a year at that point. Every time it ran, the Cavs were reminded of the loss. They wanted to take us down more than any other team that year. The Cavs came out strong and controlled the tempo in the opening games of the third round. It was a back-and-forth series until we figured out how to defend against Lenny Wilkins's slow-moving half-court offense. Cliff Levingston and B. J. Armstrong proved clutch with important baskets in final moments of key games. The Cleveland series was tougher than expected, but we continued to show that we were survivors. Jordan was awarded the league's MVP for the second straight year between our matchup with Cleveland and the finals against the Portland Trail Blazers.

In game one against the Blazers Terry Porter came out tough, making his first seven shots. Not to be outdone, Jordan hit six consecutive three-pointers and gave the crowd his famous shrug after the sixth. We won by thirty points and thought we would breeze through the remaining games and repeat. But Clyde Drexler, Jerome Kersey, Kevin Duckworth, and Danny Ainge had other ideas.

Portland threw everything they had at Jordan the second game, double- and triple-teaming him. Clyde Drexler helped take the Chicago crowd out of the game with a few incredible aerial shots to propel the Blazers to an early lead. Jordan, showing his leadership, did not try to force his shot and instead looked for the open man, but he still managed thirty-nine points just as in game one.

When Drexler fouled out of the game we thought we had it locked up, but Danny Ainge and Terry Porter teamed up for a spectacular comeback in the final minutes of the game to send us into overtime. Jordan received a technical foul that changed the tide of the game for good. Game two, which we should have won, slipped out of our hands. We were overconfident and paid a price.

Entering into the finals, I had not actively encouraged other players to boycott any of the games as I had the year before, against the Lakers. After this season I would become an unrestricted free agent.

My first choice was to finish out my career with the Bulls. The knowledge I had of the triangle and my consistency off the bench when the team needed a three, as well as my success at the three-point competitions, made the prospect of going elsewhere unthinkable. Even if I weren't picked up by the Bulls, I had practiced nearly every day with Michael Jordan, the best player in the league—possibly in the history of the NBA—and had played with a team that would win two straight championships. Adding that up, and considering that I was in the best shape of my career and a major threat from behind the arc, everything appeared to signal a big payday after this season. So I had to keep the reins pulled in on my politics, figuring I could pounce the next year when I had more security under my belt.

That was until a reporter put a microphone in front my face after game two and asked me about the lack of Black owners in the league. The *New York Times* ran the following piece the next day:

CHICAGO, June 4—A day after scoring 39 points against Portland, Michael Jordan took a different sort of shot this afternoon—from one of his teammates.

Craig Hodges, the Bulls' 3-point shooting specialist and one of the league's best, chided Jordan and other National Basketball Association players for failing to use their visibility to call attention to pressing social and political issues, from the deepening plight of inner-city youth to the failure of owners to hire more black head coaches.

Hodges spoke after the other Bulls had left practice for the day, and Jordan could not be reached for comment.

The 31-year-old Hodges, who has chided Jordan in the past, called Jordan's lack of response to the recent violence in Los Angeles a typical maneuver to avoid controversy.

'You Are Bailing Out'

"When they came to Michael after the L.A. deal went down and asked him what he thought, his reply was that he wasn't really up on what was going on," Hodges said. "I can understand that, but at the same time, that's a bailout situation because you are bailing out when some heat is coming on you. We can't bail anymore.

"I'm not going to tell Michael what to do," Hodges continued. "At the same time, I cannot go talk to young kids and not use Michael as an example of what is possible because he has so much and he has children in the palm of his hands."

Hodges's comments came when he was asked about the lack of black head coaches in the N.B.A., which is heavily populated with black players. Only two head coaches are black. Hodges said he had suggested to some players that they consider sitting out a playoff game in protest.

Onus on the Players

"Twelve jobs come open and none of us gets one. That's drastic," Hodges said of the recent head-coaching vacancies. "It's also drastic for us to say 'We're going to stop working.' But nobody is going to do that. The problem is that we are apolitical and we are not unified."

Hodges said he intended to be more critical of fellow players than of owners. He said he felt that it is the players who are shirking an obligation at a time when increasingly they are being looked to as beacons of light.

"This is a war," he said. "We're in war when you look at what happened in Los Angeles, what's getting ready to happen in Chicago, Newark. The poverty in the city is so hellish, just look across the street. Then you have us playing in here—how much money did we make here last night? How many lives will it change?

"Leadership in America is the athletes and entertainers. That's why I feel I have to start speaking out. I don't like to, I don't like to step on toes. I don't feel like somebody should tell you what you should be doing.

"On one hand, being in this league, you have a right to make as much as you can make, but you have a responsibility. A lot of us don't look at the responsibility end of it as much as we do our right to ask for as much as we can get."

Clyde Drexler, the Trail Blazers star, said he agreed with Hodges. He said the absence of blacks as head coaches is a particular problem.

"We talk about it all the time," Drexler said. "Eventually, I

LONG SHOT

think something has to be done. At some point in time, something has to be said on a national level.

"I think the implication is that you can play, but you can't coach or scout or be a G.M., and I think those things need to be addressed."

Asked how he felt about sitting out a game, Drexler said:

"I think that's more of a strike situation, and I don't think you want to get into forcing anybody's hand. I think you want it to be voluntary."

I couldn't hold it in anymore. Another reporter asked me about the King verdict specifically. I responded, "Can you imagine the instant impact we could have had if, say, we had walked off the court and said, 'We want justice for Rodney King?'"

The world was watching, and I couldn't "bail out" simply in hopes of securing a contract the next season. Too much was at stake for our community. The seams were popping off, and I saw the possibility for real change in this country at the moment. The players in the NBA could have helped lead the charge.

Flying to the All-Star game a few months prior, Michael had said to Scottie Pippen and me, "You know, Clyde Drexler is just as good as me. But he doesn't know how to play the game."

"What do you mean?" I said, knowing what he meant but wanting Jordan to say more.

"He doesn't know how *to play the game*," is all Mike said before he changed the topic.

I knew Michael was talking about the rule never to talk politics, but I hadn't really spoken to Clyde about the issues. Clyde had stepped up in the *New York Times* article. Only then did the full impact of Jordan's comments on the plane hit me. Clyde will always have my respect, not only as a player but as a person, too.

I was expecting major fallout from the article at practice later that day. Jordan acted like it never ran. He wasn't about to show his cards. Jordan never backed down from a challenge, though, so I knew it was only a matter of time. Competition is what he lived for. But we had a championship to win. I kept quiet, too.

Game three, Phil talked about building a circle around ourselves to not let anything distract us from victory. John Paxson found his zone, like Michael had in game one, and we coasted to victory, regaining our confidence and the relaxed feeling that Phil encouraged in us. We faltered with sloppy play in game four. Maybe we were too relaxed; it's a fine line between relaxed and tired. We broke out to take an early lead, but the Blazers' Cliff Robinson and his "Uncle Cliffie" red headband wouldn't allow us to hold on to it. The series was tied, two games to two.

We came back hard in game five. Scottie showed Drexler he had his own talent in the air on a few occasions and brought the house down with some monster dunks. There were no wasted possessions. Jordan hurt his ankle and sat longer than we would have liked. Led by Scottie, Horace, and John Paxson, the rest of the team elevated their game and built up a sizeable lead. Jordan came back on the court with a bandaged ankle and hit a game-sealing three late in the fourth. We were up three games to two.

Game six was back in Chicago. In the locker room we all vowed that we wanted a championship win in front of our fans, whom we considered the best in the league. A win would make us only the fourth team in NBA history to win back-to-back titles. We were also eager to be done with what had been a long, grueling season. The Blazers came out strong. Jerome Kersey dominated the first quarter and battled fiercely with Pippen. We were down 79–64 entering the fourth quarter.

Jamaal would tell me after the game that the color commentators thought we didn't have a chance and that a game seven seemed inevitable. Bobby Hansen hit a big three and made an urgent steal that brought the crowd roaring back to life while Jordan sat. Stacey King nailed what turned into a momentum-changing jumper and the bench could see the light reflecting off our second NBA championship trophy. Before we knew it we were on a fourteen-to-two run. Phil sent Jordan back into the game to seal the win.

Game six against Portland is largely considered one of the greatest comebacks in NBA Finals history. And we did it at home. But I'd sat during the moment I wanted to be on the court the most. As happy as I was for the team, I knew I'd deserved to be in the game in those final minutes. Because Bobby made his shots, no one questioned Phil's decision. My comments in the *New York Times* article ran through my mind over and over as I sat on that bench. The final word was being spoken by the higher-ups in the organization; maybe Jordan even had something to do with my lack of play. If they couldn't silence me in the press, they would shut down my game.

Jordan hopped on the scorer's table and pumped his fists in victory just like in Los Angeles. We had won two straight championships. The team and our fans were ecstatic. After the game Crawford Richmond grabbed me and said, "Let's go to Rush Street and party!"

I said, no, we were going to midnight basketball. Part of me didn't feel like celebrating with the rest of the team. We had hundreds of Bulls championship shirts in boxes in the locker room. Crawford and I drove to the Chicago Housing Authority's midnight basketball league. The kids were ecstatic—they couldn't contain their enthusiasm. Those T-shirts and I shut down every game that was playing at the Cabrini Green projects that night.

CHAPTER 17

CUT

On July 1, 1992, sixteen days after we won our second NBA championship title, I became a free agent. Nine days later, the Bulls released me. Jerry Krause called to break the news. "Craig, unfortunately we have to let you go . . . Thanks for looking after B. J., Stacey, Scott, and the younger guys on the team." The call knocked the wind out of me. As much as I'd told myself this might happen, nothing could have prepared me for it. Trades were a part of life as a professional athlete, but being released from the Bulls hurt. It felt unnatural.

I knew Jordan and the Bulls weren't going to ignore my comments in the *New York Times*—the country's "paper of record." My game wasn't any different in 1992 than on the day I signed with the team in 1989. My overall skills, speed, and certainly my jumper hadn't left me. It's easy to gauge your talent when guarding Michael Jordan every day in practice. I expected to get a call similar to the one I'd received from Tom Enlund when Milwaukee traded me to Phoenix. I knew management thought I was corrupting the minds of the players and compromising relationships with corporate sponsors. Certainly Michael wanted me gone. And

171

my controversial visit to the White House the previous fall hadn't helped my cause.

I'd turned down larger offers from other teams when I signed with the Bulls so I could be closer to my family and fulfill that life-long dream to play for Chicago. My hope was that I would finish my career with the best team in the league—the team I grew up watching and cheering for.

Forward thinking won the day, though. For four years, I'd played with and against the two best players in the world. I'd won two NBA championships and three straight three-point contests. Second to Tex Winter, I understood the triangle offense better than anyone in the league. I knew what went on behind the curtain of an eventual six-time world championship team. I was valuable. One of the twenty-eight teams in the league would offer me a contract and see me as more than a babysitter for younger players, as Krause had alluded—I was certain of it. I agreed to give Carlita my severance package from the Bulls, $80,000 a year for five years, as a divorce settlement. That is how confident I was in my future with the league.

Part of me was excited about moving on, too. As long as Jordan didn't want to play point guard—Phil wasn't about to force The General to do anything—I would have remained his back up. I longed for the days when Doug Collins ran me at the two-guard position, when I was scoring eighteen points a game. I had little doubt that I could replicate those numbers on another team. Besides, I was well respected and liked by just about every player in the league. I'd settle in somewhere.

The contract between Bob Woolf, my agent, and me was set to expire with my contract with the Bulls. Bob, who represented some of the biggest names in the business including Larry Bird and Julius Erving, as well as acts such as the New Kids on the Block, said he had too much on his plate and wouldn't be able provide me with the time I deserved. I found that a little strange, but reasonable. A Boston native, Bob worked tirelessly for his players and had earned a lot of respect in the NBA. He'd fought hard for me in prior negotiations, and he'd taken it in stride when I turned down larger offers to sign with the Bulls. "[Craig] showed a lot of loyalty to the Chicago team because that is where he wanted to be," Bob told the *Chicago Tribune* in 1989. Sure, I was disheartened with Bob's decision, but if he couldn't be there for me there must be a good reason for it, I told myself.[12] So I didn't question him beyond that. Of course, the timing couldn't have been worse. Now I had to find an agent before I could find a team.

I personally called each of the most respected agents in the NBA. No one would return my calls. Anxiety set in. My thought was that David Falk had put a bug in the ears of the other agents. Was this retaliation for my refusal to be Falk's rubber stamp as players' union president, or my endorsement of the Nike boycott, or my vocal support of the pension amendment, or the *New York Times* piece where I said Jordan was bailing out on the Black community? I thought it was probably all of the above. The agents talked to the owners more than the players did. It was a tight community, and I had committed many cardinal sins. I wasn't *playing the game* the way Jordan thought it should be played. No, I wasn't playing the corporate game.

I followed my conscience and observed the obligation I felt toward my forebears and my community, each of my ten years in the league. I knew there would be consequences; I understood the price Black leadership paid in America, but somehow I thought that in a league comprising 75 percent Black players, I would get away with it. I was wrong. Now it was time to pay the price. It was the agents who shut me out of the league first.

Desperate, I asked my longtime friend Crawford Richmond to represent me. Crawford worked at a packaging company and had no prior experience or league connections. He had a strong work ethic, though; more importantly, I could trust him. Crawford and

I shared the same commitment to Black liberation, we had known each other since high school, and he let me crash at his apartment in the city on nights I didn't want to drive back to the suburbs after games. Crawford had also traveled along with the Bulls and the Bucks on road games and to a few of the All-Star games with me. He was a familiar face around the league.

Crawford sent an elegant and persuasive letter to every owner in the NBA, touting my abilities and basketball know-how. Players with my résumé could expect a contract or at the very least an invitation to work out with a team. Coaches recognize that players can be underutilized depending on the depth of squads, and the Bulls, more than any team in the league, had depth. We didn't receive one reply. The summer dragged on. Crawford drafted a batch of follow-up letters. Crickets.

Later, Ira Berkow from the *New York Times* asked Phil Jackson why teams weren't returning my calls. Phil said, "I had the highest regard for Craig. . . . He was a great team player, never caused any problems and I respected his views. I'm a spiritual man, and so is he. I also found it strange that not a single team called to inquire about him. Usually, I get at least one call about a player we've decided not to sign. And yes, he couldn't play much defense, but a lot of guys in the league can't, but not many can shoot from his range, either."[13]

In April of that year, I was invited to the Black Expo in Indianapolis as a featured speaker on the topic of Black liberation. After giving a well-attended speech about the challenges facing the Black community and the importance of understanding Black history, I found myself sitting backstage in the VIP section of the Miss Black America contest—part of the Black Expo program—with none other than Jim Brown, whom I had met the year before in LA. T'Keyah Crystal Keymáh, who knew Jim from Hollywood, sat down alongside us. T'Keyah had been first runner-up in 1985, and she and Jim were at the Expo as contest judges.

T'Keyah was now wildly popular as an actress on the show *In Living Color*. She was beautiful, whip-smart, and funnier than hell. Her impersonations of Diana Ross, Downtown Julie Brown, Whoopi Goldberg, and Barbra Streisand had me rolling on the floor. T'Keyah and I hit it off right away and began spending a lot of time together, with her commuting back and forth between Chicago and Los Angeles. A renegade in the entertainment business, T'Keyah was conscious of the challenges that African American women faced in Hollywood, yet she wasn't about to compromise her standards to succeed in the business. She often turned down roles that required her to hide her natural hairstyle or felt too stereotypical of Black women. She walked the walk, and her popularity on *In Living Color* only continued to grow.

T'Keyah also worked as hard if not harder than I did to build Operation UNITE. The limbo state I was in with the league, however, increasingly meant that my head was in the clouds most days. I certainly wasn't giving her the attention she deserved.

That August, the relationship ended in ruin when Carlita confronted T'Keyah at DePaul University, where I was hosting a charity All-Star game. Carlita and I had been on better terms since the divorce was finalized, so I had encouraged the boys to spend more time with her. I knew the kids were better off with their mother in their lives than without, and there seemed to be a healthier distance between us now. However, both boys had mentioned that their mom was jealous of my relationship with T'Keyah. Their comments should have been a red flag. Unfortunately, my focus was being pulled in dozens of directions at the time, and I ignored the warning.

Before the game, while I was in the locker room, Carlita approached T'Keyah—they had never met—and demanded she leave the gym, never to see me and the kids again, in less than polite language, I'm told. T'Keyah stormed out of the building before I could attempt to talk to her. I arrived home after the game and all of her possessions had been removed. She had a friend remove every scrap of paper of hers from UNITE's Chicago Loop office as well. I don't blame her for leaving. I wouldn't want that drama in my life either. It would be years before T'Keyah and I saw each other again. I was heartbroken.

Losing a woman as extraordinary as T'Keyah couldn't have come at a worse time. The house in Northbrook was about to be liquidated by court order as part of the divorce settlement, as was the farm in Walkerton, Indiana. I was returning to my mom's house in the south suburbs of Chicago, and the phone was still silent. A murky depression was trying to pull me under. I was determined, however, to keep my head above water. The call would come, I told myself. I was only thirty-two; I had a lot more basketball in me. I couldn't forget that.

The leaves began changing colors, and soon the trees were bare, which for me signaled game time. The 1992–93 season tipped off in November as the Bulls were on their way to a three-peat. Trent Tucker filled my slot with the team. I have nothing but love for Trent, but he wasn't the shooter I was. Sitting out the season might have been easier if I hadn't been stuck in Chicago. The Bulls were front-page news, as they continued to dominate the league. More than anything I wanted to be a part of it. Every time I turned on the news or saw a paper I was reminded that I wasn't a Bull anymore.

My sons were both nearly teenagers and loved basketball as much as I did. So I sat with them and we watched all eighty-two games. I continued to explain the technical side of basketball to them. I couldn't deny my boys my knowledge of the game, and the Bulls were a great teaching resource. Plus, I refused to sour the good memories the boys had of my time with the Bulls. They were still extremely proud of me.

In my darker moments I would sit alone and wonder what life would have been like if I'd tried to "play the game" and only enjoyed the privileges that came with being a professional athlete on a world championship team. What if I'd pretended I wasn't Black and ignored the obligation to my people, my responsibility to them? As much as I tried not to succumb to such thoughts, my mind continually drifted in this direction. One night, my Grandma Dorothy walked in on me as I was staring at the wall in the dark living room.

"What's wrong, Craig? You've been down in the dumps for days now."

"If only I hadn't spent so much time thinking about our people and focused on my game, Grandma. . . . I'd still be on that court helping the Bulls win another championship."

"We raised you to step up when you saw something to stand on, Craig. You know that. We always encouraged you to speak out when you brushed up against a wrong. And you may have been early, or you may have been late, but you seized your moment. You made the choice to line your career up with your values. You followed the plan God laid out for you."

"Yeah, but for what? The world is no better for what I did."

"How do you know who you did and didn't inspire? I know for a fact that kids look up to you, and not only for what you did on the court. You know that as well as I do, Craig."

I sat in silence.

"Do you remember crying the night Martin Luther King was killed? You were eight years old and I remember it like it was yesterday. You didn't know Dr. King from Adam, but you knew how much he meant to your mom and aunts. You felt their pain deeply. You lived his death through them. That day changed you, Craig. You recognized at an early age that children living in all the houses out there love their families just like you love yours. You never lost sight of that. You are a fighter, Craig. You always have been. And your fights have been for all the right reasons. I can't tell you how proud I am of you because of that."

I felt a calmness and a clarity settle over me as I listened to her. My grandma had a way of filling me up with life, and she motivated me to continue on. She and my mom and aunts and uncles were there for me when I needed them most.

* * *

My name appeared in the papers again in early January when the votes for the All-Star team were being cast. Reporters asked if I would be allowed to defend my three-point title. The official word from the NBA front office was that I would be barred from the competition because I was no longer part of the league.

Sam Smith from the *Chicago Tribune* called me for my thoughts on the matter. I reminded Sam that Magic Johnson was invited to play in the All-Star game in 1992, and Rimas Kurtinaitis from the Soviet Union was invited to be an extra participant in the three-point contest in 1989. Neither played in the league, so there was precedent for me to shoot. Sam reported what I said and others ran with it. Soon after Sam's piece ran, the NBA operations director, Rod Thorn, called the decision to keep me out of the competition a "mistake." Players such as Mark Price from the Cleveland Cavaliers protested my inclusion. I beat Price the previous three years, so his complaints were unsurprising.

I received the official invitation in mid-January, with a little over a month to prepare. It was up to me to figure out where I could get back to competition-ready shape. So I shot in my mom's driveway and at a local church's gym. Sixty miles separated the cracked driveway and the Berto Center in Deerfield, where I'd prepared for the competition the previous four years with the Bulls, but the distance felt even greater. Needless to say, the church gym and the driveway were no substitute for an NBA practice facility. Despite the less-than-ideal conditions, I shot day and night for those few weeks. This could be my last opportunity to prove I still belonged in the NBA, I kept telling myself.

My kids and I arrived in Salt Lake City a day before the competition. As we stepped off the elevator at the hotel, Dominique Wilkins walked toward us. I waved. The last time Dominique and I had spoken, he and I were laying the wreath on Martin Luther King Jr.'s gravesite. "The Human Highlight Film," as Wilkins was nicknamed, dropped his eyes, turned, and walked in the other direction.

"Come on kids, let's get to our room," I said, already feeling disillusioned less than an hour after arriving in Utah. What was being said about me? I was confused.

Charles Barkley approached me during warm-ups later that day. "I know what you are going through, man," he said, as he sorrowfully patted my back.

"If you know what's going on, then speak about what you know, Chuck," I said. But Barkley walked off without saying a word. Now I really wondered what was going on. I had been expecting a reunion, and all I found was cold shoulders and coded messages. I felt like I was floating in the middle of the ocean in a radioactive boat with no oars. I did my best to focus on the competition and let it all roll off my back, but it was a challenge.

I'd packed a black uniform with the gold letters "UNITE" on the front of the jersey for the competition. "No, no, Craig, we have a uniform for you," said a league representative as he handed me a generic NBA uniform without a team logo. *I'd be shooting for the owners, apparently?* I wanted to pick my battles wisely at that point, so I changed out of my UNITE uniform without protest.

The media swarmed me before the competition. Sam Smith asked me what I would have done if I hadn't been invited to participate. "I'd have been outside with a banner that read, 'Paper Champ.'

I'd have been out there like Ali, yelling, 'Paper champ, paper champ. They ain't the real champ,'" I laughed. I kept things light as best I could, maintaining hope that I would be picked up by a team after the shootout. But invoking Ali, who was denied the ability to compete and stripped of his title for refusing to fight in Vietnam, was my own coded message.

As luck would have it, Mark Price and I were matched up in the first round. I missed short on my first two shots and the money ball and never recovered, managing only fourteen points. Price scored twenty. My score was enough to move me into the next round, though. In the semifinal I fared better, with sixteen points, but I finished third in the competition behind Price and Terry Porter. The whole experience never felt right. A creeping sense of embarrassment proved hard to shake. The interactions with Dominique and Charles and a general frigidity from the rest of the players made me feel like a pariah that weekend.

The question of "manhood" has always loomed over African American men. In many respects the NBA was one of the only places where African American men could gather and feel like men are "supposed" to feel: strong and respected. "I Am A Man" was written on the placards worn by the mostly Black striking garbage workers in Memphis the day Dr. King was killed in 1968. Playing in the NBA, Black men didn't need to worry about questions as basic as "Am I a man?" It took being kicked out of the league for me to realize how insulated I had been from that question and its deeper meaning. Yes, my family and God gave me my true strength, but the league made it much easier to display. I began to understand why few players spoke up. It was more than the money and the adulation: it was the luxury of feeling secure and strong as a Black man—as long as you played the game, of course.

CHAPTER 18

BUZZER BEATER

Melancholy was grabbing me tighter. I felt like I was suffocating each morning when the alarm went off. I would drive the boys to school, then return home and sit under a lamp with curtains drawn, reading, looking for answers to what was happening to me until I had to pick the boys up again. A sour feeling coursed through my veins. Books kept me distracted. They calmed me, placing my struggle in the larger framework of history and giving me perspective. So many other people had endured greater hardships fighting for justice. Relative to those who had died fighting for their freedom, what I was experiencing was small. I had to keep reminding myself of that. For my boys, I had to stay sane.

At home one day I received a phone call from a staff member at Jesse Jackson's office. "Craig, Nelson Mandela is coming to Chicago, and Mr. Jackson is hosting a fundraiser. Would you like to come and meet him?" I nearly fell out of my chair. This would be Mandela's first and only visit to Chicago after being released from prison after twenty-seven years. Of all the people he could meet in this city of 2 million people he wanted to sit down with me.

Mandela was a huge basketball fan, and he loved the Bulls. He knew about my political activity and requested I attend the lunch. I had followed the developments in South Africa closely ever since Arthur Ashe brought apartheid to my attention. The day Mandela walked out of prison on Robben Island in Cape Town was further confirmation of what I had been taught by my mom and aunts. The former political prisoner was now running for president of the state that had held him captive. The impossible was possible when enough people rallied behind a cause.

My family was overjoyed when I told them about the lunch. I was one of twenty-five people invited to the event, and the only athlete. Everyone else was a formal political or religious leader. Name cards sat on polished white plates in the dining room at Operation PUSH headquarters. I walked around an oval table looking for mine and realized I was seated next to Mandela. My card was to his left, and Jesse Jackson's was placed to his right. A sense of validation came over me when I looked down at those name cards.

People began filtering into the space, and Mandela was the last to arrive. A giant smile filled his face when he saw me. He hugged me and we sat down—he actually knew who I was. There are times when you can't help but wonder if there is a greater plan for people when they stand up for justice. Despite the challenges of the previous months, my life was on the right path.

Mandela addressed the crowd and discussed the changes happening in South Africa, expressing how thankful he was for our support. The international boycott, divestment, and sanctions movement against South Africa had played a huge role in bringing down apartheid and winning his release. For Mandela everything revolved around solidarity and organization in the face of injustice. He affirmed everything I believed in.

After the speech he sat down, and others began to compete for his attention. *For someone who spent nearly three decades in prison he carries himself with a lot of grace,* I thought. Mandela had a near-messianic quality about him. He addressed everyone at the table individually. He had a way of slowing people down when they tried to fill the space with their own egos or tried to monopolize discussion. Mandela could raise money without coming across as fake, which amazed me. He trusted the line he walked. Truth gave him his power. He didn't need to be anyone other than himself.

I spent the rest of my summer working with kids and did my best to inspire others the way Mandela inspired me.

✳ ✳ ✳

Anxiety over my career reached peak levels in the winter of 1994, my second full season without a team. Every day I wasn't on the court was another day that made a comeback feel more unlikely. Late the following summer, an offer to play for Clear Cantù in Italy came through. It was a relief, but I would have to leave my boys. We had been through so much by then that the thought of it broke my heart. I had little choice if I wanted to keep the lights on, though. I signed a one-year deal for $125,000 to play in Italy, a fraction of what I was worth in the NBA. Maybe this would be my opportunity to show the league I was still game-worthy. In Italy I thought about nothing other than playing basketball and averaged thirty points per game as shooting guard.

After the one season with Clear Cantù I returned to the States, confident that my numbers in Italy would pique a team's interest. Again, no agents returned my calls or replied to the letters Crawford sent, highlighting my impressive showing overseas. Italy has one of the most competitive leagues in the world. How could anyone deny my abilities at that point? The phone never rang.

The claws of depression began to grab hold of me as my bank account slowly circled the drain. I didn't invest my money in con-

ventional ways. Everything I made I gave back to the Black community or to Carlita. I never bought fancy cars or extravagant houses.
I tipped recklessly; I had the habit of leaving a $100 bill on $30
meals. Other than that, I lived a simple life for the most part. The
Black community was my retirement plan. I believed in the Golden
Rule. If I invested in the community, I trusted that I would be taken
care of. I was young, idealistic, and unrealistic.

I took a job with Chicago State as a head coach after it became
evident that no agent or NBA team was going to call me back. That's
when the depression turned to anger. I hired a lawyer and sued the
NBA for racial discrimination. From a distance few understood
what I was trying to do. The lawsuit was never taken seriously because I didn't have the money to compete with the NBA's lawyers. I
had a case—I just couldn't afford an attorney of the caliber needed to
take up the difficult and expensive task of proving that a league with
a large majority of Black athletes could discriminate based on race.

I lost the suit and lost the energy to coach full time. Chicago
State fired me after only two seasons. And I'll be the first to admit I
deserved to be fired. The depression floated back over me like a dark
cloud. I'd drop my kids off at school each morning and go back to
bed, but I'd always get to up to play at least some basketball each day.
My kids would see me score forty in a summer-league game and ask,
"Why aren't you hooping, Dad?" I never knew what to tell them.

Tim Grover, Michael Jordan's trainer, owned a gym with Jordan on Randolph Street in the West Loop of Chicago. I took my
sons there because I knew the top talent in the league was playing in
preparation for their own NBA careers—Antoine Walker, Michael
Finley, and others all showed up. Before long, though, Tim Grover
approached me and said, "You can shoot here for the rest of the day,
but this gym is only for my guys."

"There are only two world champions in this gym, me and
Richard Dent, and you want to kick me out?" I replied in disbelief.

"Sorry, Craig, but this is the way it has to be."

I came back the next day and was stopped at the door by security. "Mr. Hodges, you aren't allowed in the gym anymore," said the guard. I looked him in the eyes, nodded, and left with my sons. I remember an unseasonable chill in the air as we walked to the car. My world was changing. I felt embarrassed driving home with Jamaal and Jibril. We didn't say much. I couldn't offer them any lessons in that moment. Their dad, their hero, was being ostracized by Michael Jordan, the most popular man on the planet.

Later that night, reflecting on the experience, I thought of the line from the Bible, "The first shall be last, and the last shall be first." Maybe being kicked out of Jordan's gym meant I was on the right path. Maybe there was a lesson in all of this for my sons and me after all. If ever those boys were going to take a stand in this world, they would have to come to terms with the isolation and consequences that follow those who challenge power. They would be stronger for this experience, I told myself.

The ramifications of speaking up in the league were reaching into all corners of my life. I wasn't touring the country the way I used to, so maintaining my far-flung Operation UNITE connections proved increasingly difficult. Eventually the organization stopped functioning as I'd intended and I was forced to close shop.

I had to sell my championship rings, my three-point trophies, and the uniforms I wore during the three-point contests at auction. I never wanted to spend too much time thinking about money. I'd seen too many of my friends lose the fire they had for basketball and for life after signing big checks. While I was in the league, I'd been determined not to lose the best part of myself to the worship of the almighty dollar. But poverty can cause great damage to the soul, too. The little bit of green I made selling my memorabilia was gone before I could blink. I had trouble paying the electric bill. Some nights my kids and I sat together by candlelight. I certainly couldn't afford to buy Jamaal and Jibril Air Jordans. I'd spend my last dollar on my kids, and that's what I did. And I would do it again. "A fool and his money will soon part," the Bible says. Unable to sleep nights, I roamed my house, this verse rolling over and over in my head.

I tried to live in the moment, as all the world's religious texts encourage us to do, but my situation seemed more complex than that. Feeling banished from your community is painful and debilitating in many ways. It wasn't that I was afraid to work or to look for a job. A six-foot-two shooting guard who can hardly dunk won't play ten seasons in the NBA if they can't get their hands dirty. The larger issue was that I couldn't function in society as I once had. I was on a downward spiral, feeling utterly alone and scared. It was nearly impossible for me to manage life outside of basketball.

I spent the next ten years hosting basketball clinics, working with underprivileged kids who lived in housing projects, and raising my boys. Somehow I managed to keep food on the table. The heartache of not playing in the NBA became less acute with time. A history book or a religious text was always within arms' reach—reading and my kids kept me going.

Tex Winter, too. He was there for me when few were. He'd call and check in on me often. "Hey, Hodge, keep your head up. Things are going to turn around for you. I can assure you of that. You understand the game of basketball too well for people to ignore you forever. If there is anything I can do to get you back in the league, you know I'll do it," he'd tell me on the phone. His words were a great comfort.

In 2005, Phil Jackson was hired by Jerry Buss to return to Los Angeles to coach Kobe Bryant, Lamar Odom, and the rest of that highly talented Laker team. Phil, who had been let go from the Lakers just the year before in an ugly breakup, began reassembling his old coaching staff from the Bulls in the hopes of adding to his ten championship rings (six with the Bulls, three with the Lakers, and two as a player with the Knicks). Tex responded to Phil's request to rejoin the Lakers by insisting I be hired on as a shooting coach, too—a job that would keep me off the bench during games and offered little opportunity for me to grab a microphone to say something controversial. Phil agreed to Tex's terms, and Tex stayed true to his word, as he always had. The triangle offense would be crucial to the Lakers' success, and Phil knew I understood the system as well as anyone in the world. "Because he actually ran the triangle in games, Craig might know the system better than me," Tex told Phil at practice one day.

To be back in the game, finally, was a tremendous feeling. The joy stemmed not only from the basketball but also from the team culture. As with the Bulls, Phil encouraged discussion and debate on topics well beyond the game of basketball. "Get the angry Black man over here," I'd hear a voice booming from the training room. It was Kobe Bryant, always up for a discussion on politics and race, who would want me to settle a dispute he was having or hear about some piece of history he had just read. Lamar Odom, whose father, Joe, ran in the same circles as Malcolm X for a time, had the most comprehensive grasp of Black history and religion on that Laker team. Alex Haley's *Autobiography of Malcom X* was Lamar's favorite book. "I hate referring to myself as 'black.' 'Black' is dark and hopeless. That's not who I am. I am the opposite of that, or at least I try to be," he'd say. Lamar, like me, saw Islam as a religion for Black people. Christianity was the religion of slave owners, a religion forced down the throats of Africans. Islam, in contrast, was our choice. We talked about this often.

Of all the players on that Laker team, Lamar and I were the closest. Lamar battled hard against his demons. He talked about how his father had died of a heroin overdose. As much as Lamar respected his father's connection to the struggle he was also scared of winding up like him. In 2015, when I heard Lamar had suffered an overdose, I tried to fly out to Los Angeles to visit his bedside, but the people surrounding him made it all but impossible. Lamar is one of the humblest people I know—a real truth seeker. His recovery filled me with relief. I wish him only the best, and I have all the confidence in the world that he will find his way.

Kareem Abdul-Jabbar was another assistant coach for the Lakers at the time. On a few occasions he came with me to Jibril's basketball games at Long Beach State. It was surreal to talk politics, religion, and life with my childhood hero. Kareem is a genius. He lives to read, write, and understand the world that surrounds him. We couldn't go anywhere without people hounding him for autographs, which makes it difficult to sit quietly and observe things, as he likes to do. We bonded over our mutual love of books, Black history, Islam, the medicinal benefits of cannabis, and social justice. *Giant Steps*, Kareem's autobiography, was a life-changing book for me and inspired me to write my own story.

I coached with the Lakers for six long and beautiful years. I collected two more championship rings with the team. My time back in LA renewed my spirit. I was my old self again. Tex and the rest of the basketball community saved me once more.

∗ ∗ ∗

In 2013, I was hired to coach the Halifax Rainmen, a professional basketball team in Nova Scotia, Canada. Soon after my arrival in Halifax, I received a call out of the blue from Steve Simon, Dennis Rodman's agent. I knew Dennis but only casually. We hadn't spoken in years. Simon explained that Dennis had spent many months in North Korea with Kim Jong-Un, the country's "supreme leader." Rodman and Kim were hosting a basketball clinic and exhibition game—framed as a diplomatic mission of sorts—and they wondered if I would be interested in playing. "You were the first person on Dennis's list," said Simon. "And you'll be paid $20,000."

"Are we even allowed to fly there?" I said, not knowing what the travel restrictions were.

"Everything will be taken care of," Simon assured me.

I knew next to nothing about North Korea, only that George W. Bush had labeled it part of the "Axis of Evil." I had an idea the country was repressive, but I don't always trust what the president or the US media tells me about which country is or isn't a force for good in the world. Who was I to say the people of North Korea didn't deserve a basketball clinic? Besides, to paraphrase Ali, no North Korean ever called me "nigger."

I agreed to play. A few months later I flew twelve hours from Halifax to Beijing. After I'd arrived in Beijing, a Chinese customs agent approached me. "Mr. Hodges, you will not be allowed to fly to Pyongyang today," he informed me. The delay of my flight out of Canada had apparently shut my window to fly into North Korea. I had a hard time understanding exactly what was going on, but I avoided making waves. I couldn't imagine the US embassy rushing to my aid in this situation. Only a few hours after landing in Beijing I was back on a plane to Halifax.

Dennis Rodman, along with Kenny Anderson, Vin Baker, Cliff Robinson, Charles Smith, Doug Christie, Sleepy Floyd, and four streetball players, played in the exhibition match. I was told that the crowd was unusually quiet during warm-ups. No cheering, no music. Minutes before tip-off, in front of 13,000 mostly silent North Koreans, Dennis grabbed a microphone, walked up to Kim Jong-Un, who was sitting courtside, and sang "Happy Birthday" to him, Marilyn Monroe–style. I nearly fell out of my chair laughing upon hearing this.

As much as I would have loved to have seen such a hilariously bizarre display in person, I now consider the twenty-four hours I wasted flying to and from Beijing a blessing. After the exhibition game all the players except Dennis flew back to the United States.

Dennis had his own itinerary, which involved boozing it up with Kim Jong-Un for a few more weeks. They say Rodman knows more about Kim than anyone in the CIA.

Rodman returned home to a media firestorm. George Stephanopoulos berated him on *This Week*, the Sunday morning talk show. "Were you aware of [Kim's] horrendous record on human rights?" Stephanopoulos asked, scolding Dennis. Dennis gave a somewhat incoherent answer. I was bothered by Stephanopoulos's self-righteousness. By selling the American public on Bill Clinton's draconian 1994 crime bill, Stephanopoulos played a part in creating the world's number-one prison state—yet here he was, lecturing a retired Black basketball player on human rights. *A hypocrite*, I thought. Nevertheless, I'm glad I never made it to that game. I can only imagine the blowback I might have experienced.

Back in Halifax, I received a call from Allan Houston, the assistant general manager for the New York Knicks. Houston was in charge of the Knicks' newly formed development league (D-league) team. He said that Phil Jackson, now the Knicks' president, wanted to bring me in to teach the D-league team the triangle. I would be head coach Kevin Whitted's assistant. Saying goodbye to a team named after inclement weather wasn't difficult, and I agreed almost immediately.

In New York it was quickly apparent that I was the only one interested in the triangle. Whitted, especially, couldn't be bothered. It was a far cry from my time with the Bulls and the Lakers, where nearly all the coaches and players saw value in the offense. There is only so much an assistant can do if the head coach isn't on board. So we lost—almost every game. Whitted was fired with only ten games left in the season. I took over as head coach, but by then it was too late to change much.

I've played overseas, in the Continental Basketball Association, and for Don Sterling's San Diego Clippers for godsakes, but the

Knicks' D-league team was by far the most unorganized and chaotic basketball environment I have ever been a part of. Most importantly I wasn't having fun; none of the players were. If a basketball team isn't having fun on the court they will assuredly lose. I never went running to Phil to complain, though. I let it play out. The team and I parted ways after only one season. I needed to come home to Chicago anyway—it had been more than ten years. It was time to reconnect with my roots.

My sons and I spend a lot of time together now. We mostly talk about basketball and the condition of Black people. Jibril averaged almost fifteen points per game at Long Beach State. He graduated the best three-point shooter in the school's history. (Of course they didn't have a three-point line when I was at the school or Jibril would have been the *second best* three-point shooter in school history!) After Long Beach, Jibril spent ten years playing basketball in Europe.

I am certain that my ouster from the NBA hurt Jibril's basketball career. He'd earned the right to play on the highest level. Jibril was never invited to the pre-draft camps, like many of the sons of my former colleagues were. There is not a bone in my body that doesn't think he deserved at least a tryout with an NBA team. We sit on the couch and watch the kids he grew up with, like Steph Curry, and talk about what things might have been like if I had played by the rules—or if others had been willing to fight with me.

Jamaal earned his business degree at Long Beach State. Now he and I are hosting basketball camps together at my alma mater, Rich East. Jamaal didn't play in college but he has a sharp mind for the game. He'll be a great coach one day. For now he helps me keep my finances in order.

I think about Tex often. He lives in Kansas City, his mind destroyed by Alzheimer's disease. Without Tex in my life I wouldn't have had the chance to major in Black Studies. Without Tex I wouldn't have played or coached on a world championship team. Without Tex

I may not have made it to the other side of my darkest days. I miss him a great deal, and I'll cry like a baby when he leaves this earth.

* * *

It was a warm and humid morning in July 2015. The sun was beating down on me. I stood in front of the black-speared fence that guards the White House, practicing reading my letter before the cameras clicked on. ESPN had flown me to Washington, DC, to film a *30 for 30* episode about my life. The words, as I rehearsed them more than two decades after they were written, still felt relevant, even urgent. A crowd, noticing the cameras and a Black dude in a white dashiki— that still fits—began gathering around me to see what was up.

Inspired by the crowd, I heard my voice get deeper and stronger. As I read, my mind drifted to thoughts of Mike Brown, Freddie Gray, and so many other young Black men and women whose lives have been taken by the police since Rodney King was beaten in 1991. I thought of the struggles of my ancestors, who were brought to this country as property. I thought of those who were debt-ridden back home, who would never have the opportunity to have their voices heard by the president of the United States. For these people, I couldn't mess up. I lifted my head again to see even more people stopping to listen. I focused more intently on the letter. *How old these words are*, I thought. Nat Turner hollered them when he rose up against his slave masters. Malcolm X preached them in the mosque. They rolled out of Muhammad Ali when he resisted the draft. John Carlos and Tommie Smith uttered them silently atop the medal platform in Mexico City. My mom and my aunts chanted them alongside Dr. King. My uncles cheered them watching Jim Brown and Curt Flood on television.

These people, and countless others like them, spent much of their lives pursuing and embracing the same old idea: justice for all people. When I finished reading I heard clapping. A part of me felt strong in front of the cameras and strangers. Another part of me felt sad and angry. *It's criminal that we still have to talk about things like racism, war, and economic inequality in the twenty-first century*, I thought. It shouldn't be like this. There is no excuse. Not in such a prosperous country that claims liberty and justice for all. Yet so many go without. So many are unheard.

I thanked everyone who had gathered. We wrapped the shoot, and I hopped a ride to the airport. Flying back to Chicago, I pulled out my phone and scrolled through photos of my sons. They were just babies when I delivered the letter to George H. W. Bush in 1991. Now they are men. I am graying. The world is different but still the same. *We are in this game together, playing for the highest stakes. I need to keep at it for them*, I thought. I'll eventually hear the final buzzer. When that happens I want my sons to know that I tried my best to do the right thing, both in and outside the family, because I want them to be inspired to pass that ball to their kids. That's how we keep this movement going, on the court and off. We owe it to the ancestors. And we owe it to the future.

NOTES

---

1   William Recktenwald, "922 Homicides Made 1991 Year to Forget," *Chicago Tribune*, January 1, 1992, http://articles.chicagotribune.com/1992-01-01 /news/9201010135_1_homicide-victim-drug-trafficking-killed.

2   Jon Greenberg, "Kristof: U.S. Imprisons Blacks at Rates Higher Than South Africa under Apartheid," Politifact.com, December 11, 2014, www.politifact .com/punditfact/statements/2014/dec/11/nicholas-kristof/kristof-us-imprisons -blacks-rates-higher-south-afr/.

3   Barry Temkin, "Finally, He's the Real McCoy," *Chicago Tribune*, December 19, 1993, http://articles.chicagotribune.com/1993-12-19/sports/9312190458 _1_real-mccoy-state-title-dean-smith.

4   Ibid.

5   Carlita has made this information public.

6   Kareem details his experiences with reporters in his excellent book, *Giant Steps* (New York: Bantam Books, 1993).

7   The United States boycotted the 1980 Summer Olympics because of the Soviet invasion of Afghanistan.

8   As cited by Sam Smith in *The Jordan Rules: The Inside Story of a Turbulent Season with Michael Jordan and the Chicago Bulls* (Simon & Schuster, 1992).

9   Curry beat the record under new rules that allowed players to score a maximum of thirty-four points instead of thirty, with the addition of a two-point money ball rack. Previous rules had only one money ball at the end of each rack.

10   Steve Aschburner, "The All-Star Game that Nearly Wasn't," Hang Time (blog), NBA.com, February 13, 2014, http://hangtime.blogs.nba.com/2014 /02/13/the-all-star-game-that-nearly-wasnt.

11   Some, including Jack O'Donnell, chief of the referee crew that game, debate whether there was contact.

12   Sadly, Bob would die of heart failure at the young age of sixty-five at his home in Hallandale, Florida, in early December 1993, a little more than a year after we parted ways. I'm sure a part of him wanted to spend more time with his family, as he possibly sensed he had only a short time left on the planet.

13   Ira Berkow, "The Case of Hodges vs. the N.B.A.," *New York Times*, December 25, 1996, www.nytimes.com/1996/12/25/sports/the-case-of-hodges-vs-the-nba.html.

INDEX

197